Forgotten Worlds

By Michio Kushi
with Edward Esko

One Peaceful World Press
Becket, Massachusetts

To the memory of Marlene Millman

Published by One Peaceful World, Becket, Massachusetts, U.S.A.

For further information on mail-order sales, wholesale or retail discounts, distribution, translations, and foreign rights, please contact the publisher:

One Peaceful World Press
P.O. Box 10
308 Leland Road
Becket, MA 01223
U.S.A.

Telephone (413) 623-2322
Fax (413) 623-8827

First Edition: April 1992
10 9 8 7 6 5 4 3 2 1

ISBN 0-9628528-4-8
Printed in U.S.A.

Contents

Figures and Illustrations

Introduction

Early one spring morning, about ten years ago, a small group of friends and I gathered at the macrobiotic center in London. I was in England for lectures at the Kushi Institute, and now that the seminar was over, a group of us had decided to visit Stonehenge. After a quick inventory of our provisions—a bag filled with nori rolls and other natural snacks—we jumped into a van and headed for Salisbury Plain. The day was bright and sunny and the drive took several hours. After being in the city for a week it was good to get out into the countryside.

During the ride, I mentioned that Michio Kushi had visited Stonehenge several years before. Michio had said at the time that the famous stone circle may have been the center of an ancient metropolis of wooden buildings that had vanished long ago. He agreed with the idea that the monument was an observatory, but felt that it was built not only to predict eclipses and mark the solstices and equinoxes, but to record the larger 25,800-year cycle of the northern skies that he discusses in this book.

Our first glimpse of Stonehenge was from a road approaching it. The stones stand in the middle of an open field. I visualized spirals of energy moving up from the earth and down from the sky toward the tightly constructed circle of upright stones. Up close, Stonehenge seemed larger than it had in pictures. I felt strong energy converging toward these silent sentinels. Several years earlier, I had visited another of the ancient sites described in this book, this time, in the Far East. The Ise Shrine in Japan represents the opposite pole of the ancient world. Stonehenge is a monument to the darkness of the night sky. Its stones come from the more yang world of minerals. Ise is dedicated to the brightness of the sun and the more yin vegetable kingdom. Its many buildings are made of Japanese cypress and have a rich golden color. The shrine was first built nearly two-thousand years ago, and is rebuilt every twenty years according to the original cosmological design. The Ise Shrine gives one a sense of the purity of nature and the importance of living in harmony with it. Like Stonehenge, it offers a rare glimpse of an ancient cosmology based on a deep awareness of natural order.

In *Forgotten Worlds*, Michio Kushi explains the meaning behind such places as Stonehenge, the Ise Shrine, and the pyramids. He presents a view of the ancient world as a time of paradise on earth; a time when a unified humanity lived in one world. He describes the cosmic cycles that govern events, as well as the global catastrophes that destroyed ancient civilizations, including the lost continents of Mu and Atlantis. Using the Biblical prophecy in Revelation as a backdrop, Michio explains the unique meaning of our time, and offers practical suggestions for creating humanity's next golden age.

This book is based on Michio's seminars on Ancient and Future Worlds and Cycles of History and Social Change presented in Boston in the early 1970s. Since then, Michio has continued to develop and expand on these themes in the Spiritual Development and Destiny seminars that he now presents at the Kushi Institute in Becket. Some of this material was published in the *Michio Kushi Seminar Report*, the *Kushi Institute Study Guide*, and *The Order of the Universe* magazine. I would like to thank the editorial and production staffs of these publications for transcribing the lecture material and completing the artwork and illustrations. I thank Gale Jack for copyediting, and Alex Jack for supervising the project. I also thank Mike Clennan and Mercedes Gallagher, of the Kushi Institute, for their support of this project, and thank Lynda Shoup and George Weil for help with typing and production.

EDWARD ESKO
January, 1992
Becket, Massachusetts

1

Seeing Through the Mists of Time

There are two ways to approach the ancient world. One is through scientific analysis, including archaeology and anthropology, and the other is through aesthetic comprehension, which is based upon what we have experienced in the past. Scientific analysis is concerned with such activities as digging up historical ruins and collecting artifacts, while aesthetic understanding is more romantic and is motivated by an idealistic dream.

Ideally, both ways should correlate with each other. We know of the city of Troy from the epics of Homer and other poets; but the scientist, Heinrich Schliemann, actually discovered and dug up a city which he believed to be Troy itself in order to prove his dream. Schliemann's story is a good example. All stories have some roots in the past; the only problem is to find how they can be proved and interpreted.

In order to accomplish this, however, science and aesthetics alone or together are not enough. It is necessary to go one step higher, to philosophical understanding. This is not the same as the philosophy of present day academic studies, but that of the order of the universe. The story of *Stonehenge Decoded* is a good example. It was generally felt that the ancient people of Northern Europe were barbarians; but Gerald Hawkins, a professor at Boston University, felt that this was not true. He proved his idealistic view by a scientific discovery; with computers he discovered that this Neolithic stone circle on the Salisbury Plain in Wiltshire, a remarkable technical achievement in itself, was actually an observatory. With his philosophical understanding, Hawkins was able to unify his scientific and aesthetic points of view.

The top scientist is always a romantic. And we, ourselves, cannot lead our studies and daily life without an idealistic dream. Without inspiration, what can we do? Our day is valueless. Novelists, poets, and artists are using this ability freely. Without philosophy we cannot judge whether science is correct or not; after several years of macrobiotic study we discover that many scientific assumptions are untrue. But in order to back up philosophy we need memory or judgment. This is not mechanical memory but a true dream. It is possible when your condition is made clean by eating the foods that ancient people ate in more or less the same way as we are practicing macrobiotics today. If you eat whole grains and vegetables, as ancient people did, you see their dream and their vision by biological reincarnation.

There are two ways of reincarnation: (1) electrical and biological bodies fuse and return to human form; and (2) when you acquire the same quality as ancient people, their dream comes back and your life has the same style as theirs. When you eat like Lao Tsu ate, you are able to understand and live like him.

In this sense, our body is something like a television that can be tuned to many different channels simply by changing food. Animal food brings the modern stations into focus, which have only been present for several hundreds of years; grains and vegetables bring the ancient channels into view, which are millions of years old.

For a person with highly developed consciousness, everything in the past and future is now and here, and this present reality includes everything.

Our body is a turning point for food and vibrations that are coming in and going out. We have a physical body, but the universe itself is our outside body. The physical body is only our inner body, in this sense. When there is harmony

8

and continuity between inner and outer, small and large, our body and the universe can become one. It is important to realize that our body is not created from the soil but from air, vibrations, and the electromagnetic field. It is not produced by a gathering of elements but from vibrations, as if a ghost suddenly appeared. If we know our spiritual origins, we realize that the theory of Darwin is not true.

There are twelve constellations placed upon the ecliptic which encircles us, and these make twelve meridians upon our body and twelve major organs and functions within it. Besides these twelve constellations, there are trillions of stars sending light and energy toward the earth. We have trillions of cells in our bodies, each with a nucleus, mitochondria, and other structures in a spiral pattern; when these spiral cells are formed, they are an instantaneous picture of the stars, the celestial scenery at that moment, a condensed form of the celestial world. When our inner and outer worlds are synchronized, any kind of memory can come back, depending upon the quality of our cells. Memory is outside of us, but whether or not we can receive it depends upon this quality.

The ancient world exists in our memory; metaphysically, you were there. We need to bring out this memory; otherwise we cannot understand the ancient world as an actual experience or feeling.

For background information necessary to understand the ancient world, we need to know how celestial and cosmological cycles have influenced history and civilization. Therefore, let us study the galactic year cycle, the axis shift, and the North Pole cycle.

Galactic Cycles

Our solar system is traveling around the center of the Milky Way galaxy. The outer edge of our galaxy is revolving at the rate of 300 km per second; to go completely around one time takes approximately 200 million years. At various times during this cycle, the solar system is sometimes more near and sometimes less near the center of the galaxy. As a result, when the solar system is farther away, it becomes bigger—a yin state of expansion. At other times, when nearer to the center, the solar system becomes smaller—a contracted yang state.

When the solar system becomes expanded, naturally the distance between the sun and the earth becomes greater. As a result, the earth receives less heat and light, and becomes colder, as do the other planets in the solar system. At the opposite time, when the solar system becomes contracted, the distance between the earth and the sun becomes less, and the earth receives more heat and radiation. When the earth becomes hotter, its surface becomes muddy and swamplike. The atmosphere becomes more humid, and plants become lush and expanded, much like tropical vegetation today.

Figure 1: The Galactic Year Cycle

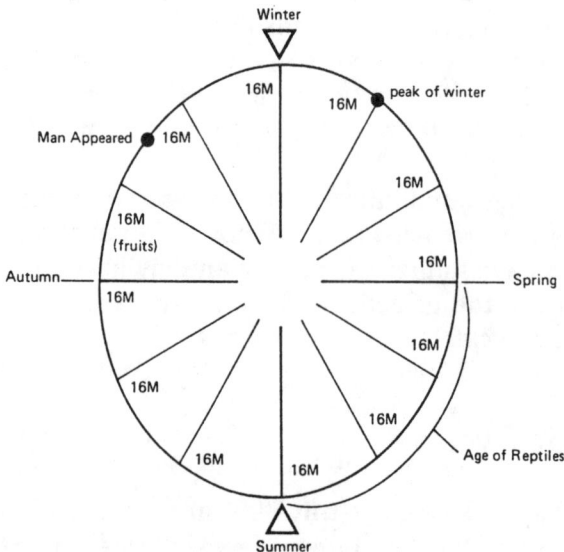

Winter

16M

16M

peak of winter

Man Appeared 16M

16M

16M
(fruits)

16M

Autumn

16M

Spring

16M

16M

16M

16M

16M

Age of Reptiles

Summer

The cycle produced by the solar system's revolution around the center of the Milky Way may be referred to as the galactic year. Like the solar year, the galactic year can be divided into seasons. When the solar system is farthest from the center of the galaxy, that time represents the middle of galactic winter. The middle of galactic summer comes when the solar system is most near to the center of the galaxy. And, of course, in between are the galactic spring and autumn seasons. The galactic cycle now takes about 200 million years to complete, but this is changing. How is it changing? It is becoming gradually shorter. But at present, it takes approximately 200 million years—100 million years yang, and 100 million years yin. Each galactic season lasts for about 50 million years.

The earth's biological history began about 3.2 billion years ago. This period of time can be divided into eight epochs: the first seven of these eight were the time of water, or ocean life. The final epoch has been the time of land life. The proportion of the time of water life to land life is approximately seven to one. In other words, about 2.8 billion years was the time of water life, and the last 400 million years has been the time of land life.

Each of these eight epochs (seven of water life; one of land life) can further be divided into eight. Accordingly, there have been 64 periods (eight times eight) since life appeared on the planet. The last one sixty-fourth of the earth's biological history is the history of the standing animals, ape and man. Does this number, 64, suggest something else to you? In the I Ching, or Book of Change, there are 64 hexagrams. Each one represents a stage in the universal cycle of change and corresponds to one of these epochs. When we study human history, including the history of the ancient world, we are studying what has been going on during the last one sixty-fourth of the earth's biological history.

We can divide this 200 million-year cycle into twelve sections, which correspond to months in the galactic year. Each month lasts for about 16.6 million years. Human history comprises two of these months, or about 32 to 33 million years. These two months, in the galactic year, go from the late fall into galactic winter. Why did human history begin during this time in the galactic cycle? At this time, the solar system was becoming larger and larger, so the distance between the earth and sun became greater. Earlier, during the summer season, which includes the Mesozoic era, there were huge reptiles—the dinosaurs—and giant plants.

As the solar system began to expand, the earth became gradually colder, and the big plants and giant fruits that developed in warmer conditions became smaller and smaller. Juicy fruits changed into fruits with covered cells; they became more and more tight. Meanwhile, the dinosaurs didn't know how to cook food, and so with this change of weather, they became extinct. Finally, in the late fall season, small grains began to appear. The species that ate these new foods began to change toward human form. Cereal grains appeared about 32 to 33 million years ago, and as a result, human beings started to come out. Before that, the atmosphere was much wetter and there were more clouds, so that there was less celestial influence and therefore simpler forms of life. When more stars began to shine upon the earth, living beings developed more cells in their bodies and brain, and humanity, with intelligence, eventually appeared. A similar pattern can be seen in the yearly cycle, as thinking becomes much clearer in the cold weather.

Before the age of cereal plants was the age of tree fruits. That age produced apes and monkeys. The grass age was before that, which was the age of mammals. Before that, in the summertime, huge plants existed; that was the age of reptiles. By the change of vegetation, in combination with the change of celestial influence, animal species changed. When cereal plants started to grow and cover the whole earth, humanity appeared and started to cover the earth. We appeared because of cereal grains (which are referred to in the Book of Genesis as "herb-bearing seeds"), and that is why they comprise our primary food.

A New World History

History can be divided into fourteen distinct ages, or epochs, extending back millions of years from the present (and immediate future) to the appearance of early man late in galactic autumn.

1. The coming age. This period lasts about 30 to 40 years, from the present into the early part of the 21st century.

2. The present age. This is the most recent 120 years of history. During this period, the United States became more international in outlook and involvement.

3. The modern age. This period began about 480 years ago and lasted for approximately 360 years.

4. The medieval age. This period lasted about 1,200 years.

5. The ancient age. During this age, the change from bronze to iron was accomplished. It lasted about 3,600 years.

The ages prior to these predate recorded history. The modern view is that people in these times were living in a primitive state. However, our ancient ancestors were far from primitive, and these periods included the establishment of several unified planetary civilizations.

6. Before the ancient age was a period that lasted for about 10,000 years. Historians think of this age as the time of change from the New Stone Age to the Early Bronze Age.

7. Prior to this period was an age which lasted for about 30,000 years. This remote period was a time during which, geologically, the last Ice Age retreated. Civilization and culture began during this epoch. As these civilizations developed, they eventually united on a world scale.

8. Before that was another epoch that lasted for 90,000 years. This period saw the development of the earliest human cultures.

9. Prior to that was an epoch that lasted for 270,000 years. It was during this time that the change from ancient primitive man to homo sapiens occurred; in other words, the ancestors of present civilized humanity appeared.

10. In the epoch preceding the appearance of homo sapiens, the use of fire began. This epoch lasted for about 810,000 years. Already, by the end of that age, more than 32.5 million

years had passed since the origin of the human species. By this time, the earth was becoming more cold, and as a result, during the last one million years or so, the Ice Ages began. The Ice Ages started during the last 1/32 of human history; until the present time we have had four periods of ice, with three intervals of warmer weather. Each cycle of hot and cold lasted 250,000 years. It was during this time that a minority of people, especially those in the cold, far northern regions, began to eat meat. Throughout history, the majority of people were eating grains and food from other plant sources, and then, during this comparatively short period, a minority acquired the habit of meat eating.

11. Prior to that was an epoch that lasted about 2,400,000 years. It was during this time that primitive agriculture developed.

12. The epoch before that lasted for about 7,300,000 years, during which cooperative society, including community life, began. At that time, the gathering of grains, beans, seeds, and other plants provided the main source of food.

13. Prior to that was an earlier epoch that lasted about 22 million years. This was the dawn of humanity, during which the appearance of cereal grains led to the development of early human beings.

14. The period prior to that lasted about 66 million years. During this long age, the transition from mammals. including apes, to mankind took place. Before that, the transition from mammals to apes occurred.

As you can see, the macrobiotic view of history goes far beyond present understanding. In macrobiotic thinking, history unfolds in an orderly pattern (a logarithmic spiral) that is in accord with the order of the universe. The key to understanding the pattern of history is to discover the numerical ratios governing these ages. For example, if we take the number 32 million years, which is the total time of human history (for convenience in making calculations, we use the figure 32 rather than 33 million), and divide it into eight units, we have a ratio of 28:4, or 28 million to 4 million years. The last four million years is the time of intellectual man. It includes the time of late community life and early primitive agriculture and on up to the present.

Then, if we divide this last four million years by eight, we obtain a ratio of 3.5:0.5, or 3.5 million to 500,000 years. This is the period of civilized humanity. The last 500,000-year period began when humanity started to use fire. The discovery of fire led to the development of civilization. Then, if we divide this 500,000-year period into eight, we obtain a ratio of 437,000:62,000 years. This 62,000-year period is the most recent one-eighth of the time of civilized man. This age, which includes the present day, represents the accomplishment of civilized man, during which time, civilization developed on a planetary scale.

Poleshifts

Like a spinning gyroscope, the earth wobbles as it rotates. Over time, centrifugal force builds up, and when this expanding force reaches a peak, an axis shift occurs. An axis shift is similar to what happens when a top suddenly flips on its side and starts spinning around a new axis. A similar thing happens with ocean waves. When we view waves from the side, we see that the height of each wave is about one-eighth the distance between the crests of two waves. If there is excess motion, created by a strong wind, the usual one to seven ratio is exceeded, and the upper crests begin to billow, breaking the usual pattern.

There have been thousands of axis shifts since the earth was formed, and there will be more in the future. Unless we find some way of controlling the speed of the earth's rotation, we cannot avoid them. When an axis shift occurs, the entire process takes only a matter of days, as the shift is very rapid. An axis shift represents a world-scale catastrophe. The polar ice caps melt and a great flood is unleashed upon the earth.

Axis shifts are recorded in mythologies as great floods that destroyed civilization. Native Americans, for example, have myths and legends that talk about several great floods. One version can be found in the legends of the Hopi Indians of the American Southwest. The Hopi ate corn, beans, and squash as their staple foods, and their name means "peace." In order to understand what the ancient world was like, we need to consider the state of the world both before and after these shifts.

The Garden of Eden

Because the earth wobbles as it rotates, the earth's axis, if you imagine it extending outward toward the stars, is slowly describing a great circle in the sky. As time goes by, the star that we call the North Star changes. A complete cycle lasts 25,800 years. We are now coming to a crucial point in this cycle. In 2102 A.D., the North Star, Polaris, will come over our heads and then begin to depart.

In the half of the cycle we are coming to the end of, the earth is receiving much less influence from the heavens, because there are fewer constellations in the direction of the North Pole. As a result, the life energy of vegetation diminishes—even if the plants should appear the same—thinking declines, and it is necessary to begin hard labor as life on earth becomes difficult. In the half of the cycle that we are about to enter, there is much more influence from the sky because there are more constellations over the North Pole, and the intense energy generated by these constellations creates a richer life on earth. In the remote past, the earth was receiving these influences, and that era is remembered in mythologies as the golden age, the garden of Eden, or the age of paradise.

When the present North Star leaves the position of Pole Star, in 2102, we will begin to receive the influence from these different constellations once again, and a more prosperous time will come. About 12,000 to 13,000 years ago, celestial influence declined and paradise was lost. The North Pole pointed toward the snake or serpent constellation, and so in Genesis there is the story of seduction by a serpent and a change of food that brought about the fall of man.

Until the present time there have been more and more efforts to build up civilization, and these have reached their peak now; that is why Buddha and other teachers said that a new age would come and that we should be prepared for it. This will not be a return to the ancient world as it was, but together with the memory of this time of hardship, and by the use of the unifying principle, a new society will be created.

Figure 2: The Cycle of the Northern Sky

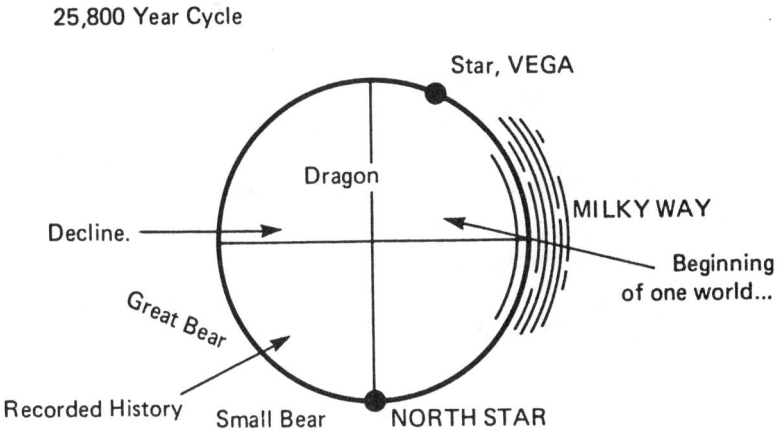

25,800 Year Cycle

Star, VEGA

Dragon

Decline.

MILKY WAY

Beginning of one world...

Great Bear

Recorded History   Small Bear   NORTH STAR

Polaris and Vega, two bright stars in the north sky, represent the two poles of this cycle. About 12,000 to 13,000 years ago, the North Pole was pointing to the star Vega, and another 12,000 to 13,000 years before that, it was pointing to Polaris. During the time when the North Pole is moving from Polaris to Vega, paradise comes to the earth. During the time when it moves from Vega to Polaris, a time of wilderness comes to the earth.

The time of paradise is a time of peace; the time of wilderness, a time of war and struggle. At the peak of the time of wilderness, humanity is threatened by fire; while at the peak of paradise, humanity experiences destruction by water. At the present time, we are being threatened by fire; 12,000 years ago, an axis shift arose, bringing forth a deluge upon the earth.

Twice in the past, humanity experienced a world scale,

17

planetary culture, or one world, and three times has experienced the wilderness of separation. We are now reaching the end of the most recent period of separation, and from now, humanity will start again toward one united world.

Wonders in Heaven

The entire cycle of the North Pole lasts 25,800 years; one-half of the cycle, 12,900 years; each section (of twelve) about 2,150 years, or roughly the length of time that Christianity has existed. As the Pole moves away from the star Vega and toward Polaris, it passes through the constellations Draco, the Dragon, Ursa Major, the Great Bear, and Ursa Minor, the Small Bear. The movement of the polar axis through these constellations is shown in Figure 3.

Figure 3: North Pole Constellations

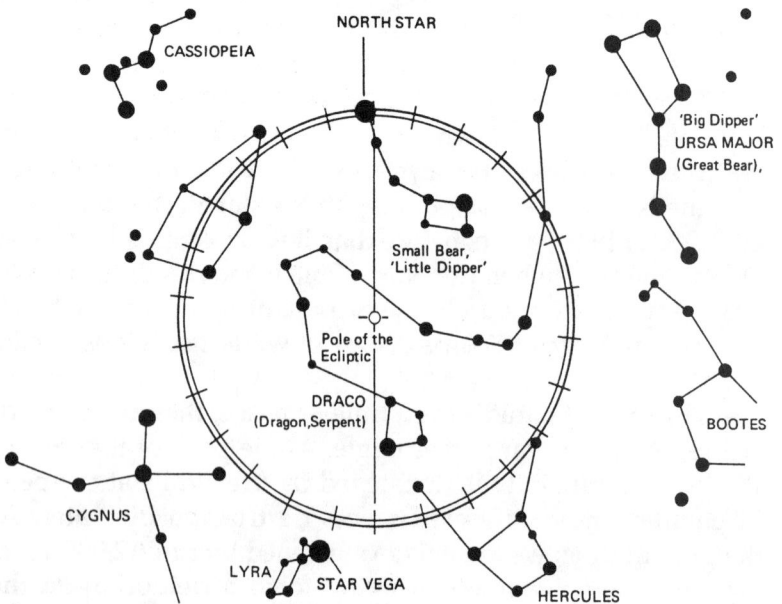

The astronomical chart of the constellations shown in Figure 3 is an example of the scientific way of study. An aesthetic description of this cycle can be found in Revelation, which is the last book of the Bible. Just as the serpent in Genesis represents the constellation Draco, the various animals and figures in Revelation correspond to these constellations, and the story which is told is an account of these movements in the sky. However, it is very difficult to interpret the last book of the Bible unless one eats very well and knows the unifying principle.

In Chapter 12 of Revelation we read: "And there appeared a great wonder in heaven; a woman clothed with the sun, and the moon under her feet, and upon her head a crown of twelve stars: and she being with child cried, travailing in birth, and pained to be delivered." The woman is the constellation of Lyra, the Harp, in which the star Vega is located. This passage describes the appearance of Lyra over the North Pole about 12,000 to 13,000 years ago.

"And there appeared another wonder in heaven; and behold a great red dragon [the constellation Draco, the Serpent], having seven heads and ten horns, and seven crowns upon his heads. And his tail drew the third part of the stars of heaven, and did cast them to the earth: and the dragon stood before the woman which was ready to be delivered, for to devour her child as soon as it was born. And she brought forth a man child, who was to rule all nations with a rod of iron: and her child was called up into God, and to his throne." The "man child" is the constellation Hercules that followed Lyra over the North Pole.

"And the woman fled into the wilderness [of space], where she hath a place prepared of God, that they should feed her there a thousand two hundred and threescore days." This period of time represents one-half of the North Pole cycle; that is to say, the time when the earth is not receiving the more beneficial influence of the Milky Way constellations. After this time is over, the golden age will begin again.

"And there was a war in heaven: Michael and his angels fought against the dragon; and the dragon fought and his angels, and prevailed not; neither was their place found any

19

more in heaven." The period of hardship was beginning on earth as the North Pole pointed away from Vega and toward the constellation Draco. "And the great dragon was cast out, that old serpent, called the Devil, and Satan, which deceiveth the whole world: he was cast out into the earth, and his angels were cast out with him." This passage describes the growing influence of Draco and the loss of paradise on earth, including the rise of deluded thinking.

"Therefore rejoice, ye heavens, and ye that dwell in them. Woe to the inhabiters of the earth and of the sea! For the devil is come down unto you, having great wrath, because he knoweth that he hath but a short time [that is, only half a cycle]. And when the dragon saw that he was cast unto the earth, he persecuted the woman which brought forth the man child. And to the woman were given two wings of a great eagle, that she might fly into the wilderness, into her place, where she is nourished for a time, and times, and half a time, from the face of the serpent." The "two wings" are the wings of the harp, or constellation Lyra, where Vega is found.

"And the serpent cast out of his mouth water as a flood after the woman, that he might cause her to be carried away of the flood. And the earth helped the woman, and the earth opened her mouth, and swallowed up the flood that the dragon cast out of his mouth." Here is a reference to the destruction by water that took place 12,000 to 13,000 years ago at the other extreme of the cycle, in contrast to the destruction by fire that threatens the world today.

Chapter 13: "And I stood upon the sand of the sea, and saw a beast rise up out of the sea, having seven heads and ten horns, and upon his horns ten crowns, and upon his heads the name of blasphemy." The beast is the constellation of the Great Bear, Ursa Major. "And the beast which I saw was like unto a leopard, and his feet were as the feet of a bear, and his mouth as the mouth of a lion; and the dragon gave him his power, and his seat, and great authority." The North Pole moved into the constellation of Ursa Major in the earliest period of recorded history, around 4,000 B.C., and remained there until about 1,000 B.C.

"And I saw one of his heads as if it were wounded to

death; and his deadly wound was healed: and all the world wondered after the beast. And they worshipped the dragon which gave power unto the beast: and they worshipped the beast, saying, Who is like unto the beast? Who is able to make war with him? And there was given unto him a mouth speaking great things and blasphemies; and power was given unto him to continue forty and two months. And he opened his mouth in blasphemy against God, to blaspheme his name, and his tabernacle, and them that dwell in heaven. And it was given unto him to make war with the saints, and to overcome them: and power was given him over all kindreds, and tongues, and nations. And all that dwell upon the earth shall worship him, whose names are not written in the book of life of the Lamb slain from the foundation of the world."

This passage describes the spread of deluded thinking over the earth. "If any man have an ear, let him hear. He that leadeth into captivity shall go into captivity: he that killeth with the sword must be killed with the sword. Here is the patience and the faith of the saints."

The Great Year

Ancient thinkers were aware of the cycles governing human events. In Greece, philosophers such as Pythagoras, Aristotle, and Plato taught that history cycles back and forth between periods of growth and regeneration and those of destruction and decay. They referred to the 25,800-year cycle of the polar ecliptic as the "Great Year," and considered it to have a decisive influence on the rise and fall of culture and civilization. Like other people in the ancient world, Greek philosophers believed that these cosmic cycles are reflections of the eternal order of the universe.

"And I beheld another beast coming up out the earth;

and he had two horns like a lamb, and he spake as a dragon. And he exerciseth all the power of the first beast before him, and causeth the earth and them which dwell therein to worship the first beast, whose deadly wound was healed." The second beast is the Small Bear, Ursa Minor, the constellation in which our present North Star, Polaris, is located. We are about to leave this group of stars, as the present North Star is at the very tip of the handle of the Small Dipper, or Ursa Minor.

"And he doeth great wonders, so that he maketh fire come down from heaven on the earth in the sight of men, and deceiveth them that dwell on the earth by the means of those miracles which he had power to do in the sight of the beast; saying to them that dwell on the earth that they should make an image to the beast, which had the wound by a sword, and did live." Our present civilization is one of fire, as can be seen in our modern world especially, where combustion is used for industry. The culmination of this is atomic fire, which threatens a world destruction opposite to the water destruction that occurred during the time of Vega. The "miracles" describe the wonders of modern technology.

"And he had power to give life unto the image of the beast, that the image of the beast should both speak, and cause that as many as would not worship the image of the beast should be killed. And he causeth all, both small and great, rich and poor, free and bond, to receive a mark in their right hand, or in their foreheads [this mark is a symbol of intoxication by modern concepts], and that no man might buy or sell, save that he had the mark, or the name of the beast, or the number of his name. Here is wisdom. Let him that hath understanding count the number of the beast: for it is the number of a man; and his number is Six hundred threescore and six." What does this number, 666, mean?

Chapter 14: "And I looked, and lo, a Lamb stood on the mount Zion, and with him an hundred forty four and four thousand, having his Father's name written in the foreheads. And I heard a voice from heaven, as the voice of many waters, and as the voice of a great thunder: and I heard the voice of harpers harping with their harps: and they sung as it were a new song before the throne, and before the four beasts, and the elders: and no man could learn that song but the hundred and forty and four thousand, which were redeemed from the earth."

The number 144,000 is representative of the importance of the number twelve, as 12 x 12 = 144. Twelve is the unit of the order of the universe; that is why there are twelve months in a year, twelve divisions in a clockface, twelve constellations of special importance, and a special word, "dozen," to signify this number. Twelve times twelve, or twelve squared, equals one hundred and forty four; and there are pictured a thousand times this number with the mark of the Lord on their foreheads. Because twelve is the number of the order of the universe, these are people who understand and live together with this order.

"These are they which follow the Lamb whithersoever he goeth. These were redeemed from among men, being the firstfruits unto God and to the Lamb. And in their mouth was found no guile; for they are without fault before the throne of God. And I saw another angel fly in the midst of heaven, having the everlasting gospel to preach unto them that dwell on the earth, and to every nation, and kindred, and tongue, and people," the "everlasting gospel" being the order of the universe, "saying with a loud voice, Fear God, and give glory to him; for the hour of his judgement is come: and worship him that made heaven, and earth, and the sea, and the fountains of waters."

"And there followed another angel, saying, Babylon is fallen, is fallen, that great city, because she made all nations drink of the wine of the wrath of her fornication." The angel is you, yourself, telling people about the order of the universe; the "hour of his judgment is come" means that now our human consciousness will develop and change the world; Babylon, the fallen city, is the mighty material civilization of the present world. After this, a new world can begin.

In the last chapter of Revelation, Number 22, the writer says, "I am Alpha and Omega, the beginning and the end, the first and the last." This means yin and yang, front and back. "Blessed are they that do his commandments, that they may have right to the tree of life, and may enter in through the gates into the city." The tree of life is the order or principle of life, with which humanity can enter the gates to the city of a new world.

When will this new age begin? The time of the fall of Babylon is now, as everyone would agree; AIDS, mental illness, and cancer are widespread. The close of the Book of Revelation is the time we are living in today. This is the last page of the Bible, which is coming to a close; the end of an age and the beginning of a new one.

This story is very beautifully, poetically explained, and covers the important points without missing any of them; the writer might have been eating better than we are, as there was no coffee at that time. It is a beautiful prophecy, an example of the aesthetic type of understanding, of which there are many.

Fire and Water

History is the story of alternating destruction by fire and water. A partial catastrophe may come soon but the great one is at the time of Vega. This is the time of stories such as the sinking of Atlantis and Mu, the time when the dragon appeared. It was also at that time, about 12,000 years ago, that Native Americans made immigrations through the Aleutian Islands.

We can trace the history of vegetable and grain cultivation until 12,000 years ago. Before that it is difficult, partly because of the catastrophe, and partly because before that time natural agriculture was used. This was an agriculture of non-tilling, non-pruning, non-fertilizing, non-chemicalization, non-weeding; non-doing, in short. Vegetables and grains today are cultivated, not wild, and so they are weak. Because of cultivation, vegetables become weak, and then the people who eat them become weak in body, intuition, and wisdom. Sickness begins on a large scale and people have illusions.

Our time is the peak of superstitions, and these have created such problems as the collapse of the family, the rise of criminal behavior, the modern epidemic of degenerative disease, nuclear proliferation, degradation of the environment, and the constant threat of war. Ancient people were free from such problems. Today's people are a totally different type of species: we must dig out our ancestor's mind, and to do this we must eat their food, erase our superstitions, and wake ourselves up to what this world should be now. Everyone is dreaming illusions; we must open our eyes and see reality.

Natural agriculture is one pole of this, and the other is monism. Monism, a feeling of oneness, as contrasted with dualism, for dualism is a feeling of separation, such as is created with nations, and other factors that constantly conflict with each other. Separation also leads to the idea of worship, for in order to worship something, one must see oneself as separate from it. Dualistic people have ideas of gaining freedom by fighting or conquering; monistic people have a different approach. Lao Tsu is a good example, as is Sun Tsu, the master strategist, who wrote about the strategy of harmony. According to Sun Tsu, the best way of fighting is to change the enemy's mind; the worst way is battle. Ancient people studied the stars and made them into symbols, alphabets, numbers, folklore, and mandalas, and we will study more of their ideas in the next chapter.

2

Forgotten Worlds

Up until 12,000 years ago, and before that for about 10,000 years, our ancestors lived in one world. At that time flying machines and other wonderful technologies were in use. The premise of the book, *Chariots of the Gods*, is more or less correct in stating that flying was going on in the past, but this was not necessarily because of people from outer space.

Suppose some great destruction should arise at the present time, on a world scale, so that modern civilization entirely collapses. Then later, our offspring would start to build up again, making gardens and so on. At that time, they would talk about former times, and stories and legends about airplanes and jet travel would be passed from generation to generation. And, thousands of years later, when our descendants had developed enough skill to dig up traces of our civilization, they would discover that in the past, there had been great things, such as the Empire State Building, the Statue of Liberty, and so forth. And they might assume that these huge structures were temples to a god or places of worship. And they would think, "Since our ancestors were primitive, they could not have built such things, so the builders probably came from another planet."

In very ancient times, some of our ancestors may have come from another planet. According to one theory, some people developed on earth, others came from other planets,

26

and the two groups intermingled. People from space brought with them understanding of how to cultivate cereal grains, together with various technologies, including the use of fire. That occurred during the age which lasted for 810,000 years. Great interplanetary migration took place at that time. Their technologies remained here and there, and somewhere in our memory, these technologies still exist. In the modern era, the Wright brothers made their airplane, Edison the lightbulb. But without memory, it is not possible to make such inventions, such creations. Imagination equals memory; memory equals imagination.

So far there have been two one-worlds. The coming one-world, which we are going to build, will be the third. The first one-world began nearly 48,000 years ago, and was made by power. The second one-world began about 25,000 years ago, and continued until 12,000 years ago, until the time when the American Indians could no longer go back and forth from this continent to the Asian continent. Before that, the Aleutians were in a warm region, and people were able to cross very easily. Similarly, in the Pacific, two continents were there, which again aided them in going back and forth. Because of the axis shift, these continents sank, cold weather came to the North Pacific, and immigration to America stopped.

The story of the flood of Noah is a combination of the memory of the flooding at the time of that shift and some local flooding in the Middle East about 6,000 years ago. That flood, in comparison with what arose with the axis shift, was much smaller.

While the first one-world was based on power (yang), the second one-world was more spiritual and philosophical (yin). During this last one-world, temples and observatories were oriented toward the heavens. The world was literally one, and their guiding principle was yin and yang. Throughout the whole world, this was the leading one.

After the wilderness began, fragments of this knowledge remained here and there throughout the world for thousands of years. About 6,000 years ago, the peak of the wilderness came—the darkest time—and humanity again started to turn toward paradise, toward one-world. At that time, people who were eating macrobiotically and who had something of the ancient cosmology and wisdom began to spread their teachings, to prepare people for the eventual time of paradise. Ninety-nine percent of the people had forgotten those teachings; they had forgotten that a united world had ever existed. But here and there, the people who had some understanding began communities and cultures.

One of the cultures that arose at that time is now under a desert in western China. Another one was the ancient upper Egyptian country. Another one was the country of the Sumerians. Another was the country of Vedanta, in the Himalayan mountains. The present country of India is based upon the thinking of Vedanta, although now it is much more fragmented. Other of these people were around the Pyrenees mountains, in what is now Spain and Portugal, and some lived in the British Islands, and later became the Celtic peoples. The Incas and Mayas were others. All of these people were more or less macrobiotic. By them, here and there, countries began, and unity began. And so, there are many legendary stories of the beginnings of those countries. Still this was the age of wilderness, so these cultures were originally built with the aspiration toward one world and one infinite universe.

However, soon the image of God, or the infinite universe, became idolized. At the same time, people who were oriented toward political power began to take over. And then, here and there, prophets and spiritual leaders came out, telling people to prepare for the coming one-world, the coming paradise, and warning them that their ways were not the best ones. All those prophets and teachers are considered, at the present time, to be the originators of present day religions, such as Judaism, Christianity, Shintoism, Buddhism, Confucianism, Taoism, and so forth.

All of those people, more or less, foresaw that the world would become one. And they saw that if things such as war and separation continued, then the time of judgment would come—the time when all the systems that make up modern civilization—so-called Babylon—would collapse. So, they warned, they prophesied.

All their prophecies, their warnings, their teachings said,

"We must know, we must return to the order of the universe; we must become aware of the one infinite universe, from which we have come and to which we are going, and in which we are living." And they said, "Do not take God as an idol." That means, do not see God as separate from you; take God as a whole, including us, including everything. And first and most importantly, we must know the law of God, the justice of the kingdom of heaven. We must know the infinite universe.

During the last period of 2,150 years (1/12th of the cycle of the Northern skies), the final warning came, from Buddha, from Jesus, from Lao Tsu, and others. Throughout East and West, these prophets started to say, "Now the time is coming, very soon. Now you really have to know and return to the order of the universe." But still, for these two thousand years, the age of wilderness has continued. Following that, their teachings were made into doctrines and huge institutions were built around them. Their teachings became mystified, and no one could understand them.

And now, after two thousand years, the turning point toward paradise is coming. The time of prophecy has passed. George Ohsawa and other people—and you—did not come to make prophecies, like Jesus or Moses or other ancient people, but came to realize them and begin the third one-world. This third one-world is to be unlike the first one, which was built by power, or the second one, which was more spiritual. In the coming one-world, we will be able to synthesize material progress with spiritual development. As a result, the forthcoming planetary culture promises to be more highly developed than both of the previous ones. Let us now study some of the traces of the ancient one-world.

Magic Squares and Circles

The magic squares are charts of the universe. They are more than 12,000 years old and are one of the few remaining traces of ancient cosmology. In Table I, every row, including the diagonals, adds to equal fifteen. Table IV is a further de-

Figure 4: Magic Squares

I

6	1	8
7	5	3
2	9	4

II

378	333	396
387	369	351
342	405	360

III

42	37	44
43	41	39
38	45	40

IV

51	6	69	46	1	64	53	8	71
60	42	24	55	37	19	62	44	26
15	78	33 (126)	10	73	28 (111)	17	80	35 (132)
52	7	70	50	5	68	48	3	66
61	43	25	59	41	23	57	39	21
16	79	34 (129)	14	77	32 (123)	12	75	30 (117)
47	2	65	54	9	72	49	4	67
56	38	20	63	45	27	58	40	22
11	74	29 (114)	18	81	36 (135)	13	76	31 (120)

velopment of Table I. It has nine major sections, each the same size as Table I; this chart has nine vibrational spheres or worlds within it. First, count from one up in Table I, and then do the same in Table IV; you will see that the same progression and direction is made. The numbers continue to move in the same pattern as you continue counting, except at the end.

Table III adds to 369. The centers in Table III correspond to those of Table IV; that is, all of the centers in Table IV make up Table III. Table II adds to 1007, which is 369 x 3. Number 41 is the center of III and IV. In ancient cosmologies, 41 is the name of the "central god." Table III adds to 123, which is the name of the prime god of movement; when we count "one, two three," we are starting to move. Lao Tsu expressed this when he said, "One produces two, two produces three, and three produces everything." All of the numbers circle around 41.

The number 369 is close to 365 1/2, the number of days in a year; it is pronounced in old Japanese as "Miroku," the "future Buddha," which means the people who understand the order of the universe represented in this chart and change the world. This number is complementary/opposite to the number 666 in Revelation. Both numbers add up to 18. The number 18 reduces to 9 (1 + 8 = 9). The number 9 is the number of fire and also of spiritual consciousness. In Revelation, 666 is used to signify destruction by fire; while in Buddhism, 369 is used to signify universal enlightenment. In Buddhist prophecy, at the time of maximum danger, when the threat of destruction reaches a planetary scale, humanity would recall the order of the universe and turn away from destruction and toward spiritual enlightenment.

Ancient people also expressed their cosmologies in the form of circles. One of these arrangements, developed more than 12,000 years ago, is known as Kanagi Guruma. When translated, Kanagi Guruma means "God's Name Tree Wagon," or the "Divine Wagon of God's Manifestation." It was also called the "Yearly Spiritual Plate," and the "Yearly Spiritual Calendar."

Figure 5: Kanagi Guruma

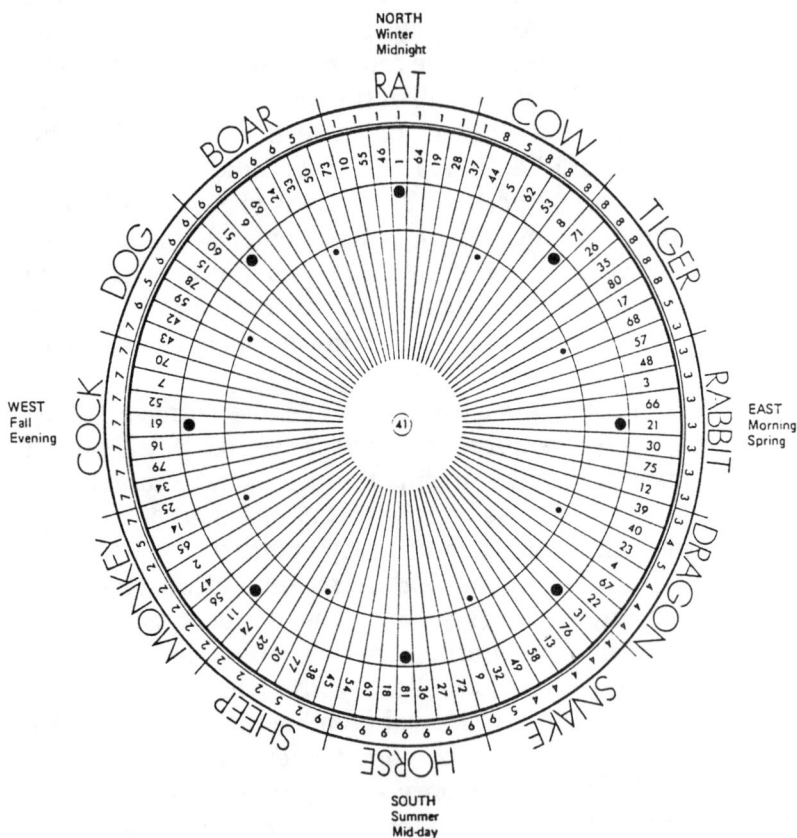

In this circle, the direction of movement is clockwise. The twelve sections of the chart correspond to the twelve divisions of the day (12 x 2 hours = 24 hours), the twelve divisions of the year, and the twelve-year cycle of Oriental astrology. They also correspond to the twelve constellations of the Zodiac, and the twelve meridians of energy in the human body. These twelve divisions represent universal stages of

32

change that arise within the continual cycle of yin and yang, or expansion and contraction. They can be found everywhere and in all things. The ancient Chinese gave each of these stages the name of an animal, such as horse, monkey, and tiger. Originally, however, the stages in this cycle were given agricultural names corresponding to the life cycle of cereal plants.

This chart also shows the four primary directions—North, South, East, and West, along with their corresponding seasons and times of day. These four subdivide into eight, and if we follow the inner set of numbers around the circle, we see that these eight stages are marked by numbers ending in one. Number 1 is the winter solstice, and also corresponds to midnight and the direction North; 71, the beginning of spring, early morning, and Northeast; 21, the spring equinox, morning, and East; 31, the beginning of summer, late morning, and Southeast; 81, the summer solstice, noon, and the direction South; 11, the beginning of autumn, or late summer, afternoon, and Southwest; 61, the autumnal equinox, evening, and West; 51, the beginning of winter, night, and Northwest. These numbers and positions are indicated by large black dots.

Kanagi Guruma, or the ancient world calendar, contains the same arrangement of numbers as the magic square. To see how this is so, go around the inner circle of numbers, adding all of the numbers together in this manner; in the Rat section, we have 10; 55, 5 + 5 = 10; 46, 4 + 6 = 10; 1; 64, 6 + 4 = 10; 19, 1 + 9 = 10; 28, 2 + 8 = 10; 37, 3 + 7 = 10. When we get a double number, such as ten, we add these numbers again; in this case, 1 + 0 = 1. The number one, then, is found in the section of the Rat. If we go all around the circle and continue this, we find the numbers arranged as in Figure 6 (see next page).

This arrangement also served as the basis for the eight trigrams of Fu Hi, and later, the sixty four hexagrams of the I Ching. Kanagi Guruma dates back to the ancient one world, and predates the I Ching by thousands of years. It was more or less a permanent calendar, with minor alterations made in it from time to time. For more information on magic circles and squares, see the book *Nine Star Ki* published by One Peaceful World Press.

Figure 6: Circle with Numbers

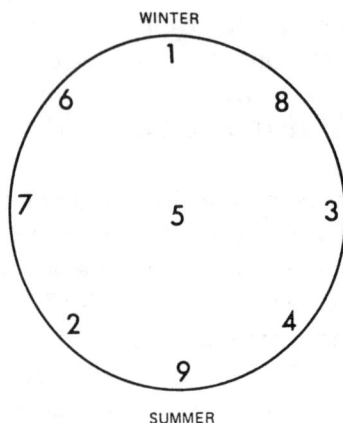

WINTER

1
6   8
7   5   3
2   4
9

SUMMER

With the same principle, but only a slightly different form, the Aztec calendar of ancient times showed all of the seasons, with the central god, corresponding to the number 41, symbolized as the god of the sun in the lower, southern, summer portion. In Tibet, these cosmological expressions took the form of mandalas. In a typical mandala, the upper portion is yin, and the lower yang, and four circles are usually arranged around a central circle. The central circles usually have 64 sections around the rim. The five circles are representative of the five transformations, or stages, of energy found throughout nature.

If we view the pyramids from the top, we can understand that they also expressed the same principle. There are many types of pyramids located throughout the world, some with a square foundation, others round. Stonehenge, when seen from the top, is another example.

Throughout the world, ancient people's cosmologies were one. Everyone followed and practiced the same principles. Their cosmologies were expressing yin and yang and they were eating grains and vegetables. Thousands of years after the ancient world perished, people began to revive the ancient understanding and used it to build structures such as Stonehenge and the pyramids of Egypt. If you study the order contained in these structures, as well as in the magic squares and circles, you can discover the wonderful cosmology of our ancient ancestors.

Government Without Power

In ancient times people lived according to a common principle. Throughout the world, they had the same understanding. There was a world community, and people felt like members of a planetary family. Leaders were not politicians but elders, like one's grandfather, and age was the basic factor in determining leadership. In the Far East, "teacher" means someone born before us; "Sensei," the Japanese word for teacher, means "before birth." There were no such words as "master." Elders were the first type of leader, and the second was spiritual or philosophical people, men or women, who were capable of understanding and applying the order of the universe in many domains of life.

Government did not actually govern in the sense of trying to control or regulate people, but provided information and education (this can still be read in the Norite, or ancient cannons of Shinto, and was called Shiroshimesu, or to "let them know"). Another function of government was to secure the basic foods necessary for life, health, mind, and spirit, and this was known as Kikoshimesu, "to hear from them," and also "to eat." This type of government could either be a central person to whom people came, or a conference of elders.

There was no idea of law or punishment or sin. Their idea of sin was that if we really did something wrong, we would get sick; the order of the universe would balance our actions, so there was no need for us to punish each other. A "sinful" person means an unhappy person, one who either actually becomes sick, has an accident, cannot do what he wants to do, or is depressed or confused. Therefore, there was no idea of sin as we have now. They also knew that unhappiness could be cured by self reflection, including change of eating, and in that sense the elders served as something like doctors or healers. People could also be cured by understanding the order of the universe; for example, by knowing that unhappiness will change and sometime in the future it will disappear. If one understands this, unhappiness disappears because we lose our attachment to it.

In order to do this, they helped the unhappy person understand what he is, and what he did was somehow against the order of the universe. Nothing more was necessary than to have the person eat well and discover his or her true self. Since there was no sin, there was no need for government by power. Present governments are based on manmade law rather than on the order of the universe, or natural law. Conflicts between countries are decided by power politics to establish sovereignty, and this will continue for awhile but eventually change as people begin to eat better and to understand true justice, which is not manmade.

The artificial structures used to govern society will eventually evolve into something else. The new government, which our macrobiotic friends are going to build, without power or rules, will be something like an educational or information center. When we speak of world government, that is what we mean. It has no big social structures, for this government is based on natural law and represents and benefits everyone. The leaders of this government work day and night for the happiness of all people.

Marriage in the Ancient World

In ancient times people were generally macrobiotic and so most of them had one husband and one wife, but this was not law. A minority had various combinations, perhaps five percent or so; they did not say anything about this, but felt that sex, like growing plants, was for the creation of life, and therefore that it was good, provided everyone was healthy and happy. There was no sense of guilt or sin in regard to sex, and like food, everyone enjoyed it. Later, after systems and social unification came out, codes of marriage were made, and today it is necessary to have the government's permission both to marry and to divorce. Before, people would just move in together and begin married life; often they would ask the opinion of their elders, and would respect this opinion. If they had had a dispute, they would just separate, and if it were settled, come back together.

This is the way of our macrobiotic movement. There are no doctrines or disciplines among us, just yin and yang; no rigid rules governing human affairs. There is a very big meaning here. This is faith; not belief, but understanding. There is a big difference. When you are young in the society of today, you make up your mind and go either toward power or toward the spiritual or religious way. But when you eat well you dissolve both and go to a new way, the order of the universe. The ancient world was like this. Since everyone was living day to day life with the order of the universe, including the world of spirit, there was simply no need for massive organizations, complicated social structures, or rigid rules governing behavior.

The Spirit of Words

To understand the Biblical saying "In the beginning was the Word," we can turn to another Biblical passage, the story of the Tower of Babel. Although this story is symbolic, it is based upon truth, because originally all people had a common way of expressing themselves, and the world had one language. Everyone opens their mouth and says "A" the same way; everywhere this is the beginning of the alphabet. In English we say "fire," in German, "feuer," in Japanese, "Hi" (pronounced "hee"). Everywhere there is the same, or nearly the same, "H" or "F" sound. When you want to find the mentality of ancient people, do not be misled by the spelling of words, but listen to their original sound.

Western babies say "mama," and so do Japanese babies. In Japanese this means baby talk asking for food, because mother is food for a baby. Actually, "mama" is the origin of the word "man." "M" is a yang, closing sound, and "A" a yin,

opening sound. Because this goes from yang to yin, it express-
es the return from the manifested world to the origin, the
spiritual world. It signifies the beginning of consciousness or
judgment, and is therefore appropriate for a baby's first
word, the first step in this course of spiritualization.

Western books open to the left; Oriental books open to
the right. Western books read from left to right, with horizon-
tal sentences; Oriental books read from right to left, with ver-
tical sentences. In English we say,"A cup of tea;" in Japanese,
"Tea a cup." In English, "I go to school;" in Japanese, "School
to go" (Gakko e ikimasu). In the Bible the first sentence reads
"In the beginning God created heaven and earth;" in the Kojiki the first sentence reads, "Heaven-earth of beginning of
time (when), high heaven field at manifested God of name is
heaven of center of God." It is confusing, something like a
puzzle. The English reading would be "At the beginning of
time in heaven and earth, in the high heavenly field the God
manifested whose name is the God of the center of heaven."

When I was working for the U.S. government as a temporary interpreter, I was asked to take a test for simultaneous
translation between Japanese and English, but I failed it, because the sentence order is completely opposite. I would have
to wait for one sentence to end before beginning the translation, but by the time I began to speak, another sentence had
begun.

Naturally, the way of thinking is also opposite. Western
thinking, typified by science, believes that unless we can see
something, or detect it with a machine, it has no existence.
Eastern mentality believes that something manifested will
soon disappear, and that anything physical is merely a shadow; what is unmanifested is considered to be real.

Because East and West have opposite languages, maybe
the middle part of the world mixes up both of them. Maybe if
we combined all languages and shook them, the average re-
arrangement would be closer to humanity's original language. From this origin, all languages separated. Or perhaps
if we recorded your voice in English, and then reversed the
tape and listened, you could not understand it, but someone
else, or someone in the past, may think that you are saying

wonderful things. At the present time everyone is speaking one-sided quick language and as yet there are no words that manifest both the infinite and the infinitesimal worlds. Ancient people had such a language, so it was simple and universal. This principle still remains in the alphabet.

God, Infinity— A B C D E F G H I J K L
1/Infinity ————M N O P Q R S T U V W X—Infinity
　　　　　　　　　　　　　　　　Y
　　　　　　　　　　　　　　　　Z

The letters Y and Z are something like extra letters which are almost unnecessary, as they sound very similar to I and C. When we look in the back of a dictionary, there are very few words under these two letters. We can see that the original alphabet had 24 (12 x 2) letters, with the first series of twelve beginning with A, which represents God, or infinity; the second series beginning with M, which represents the infinitesimal world of matter and ending with X, which is also a symbol of infinity. The letter X is a cross. It shows yin and yang crossing. In mathematics, it is used to express an unknown quantity, and corresponds to God, or the unknown one. The first and second set of twelve letters correspond to the twelve meridians, constellations, months of the year, and times of day. The alphabet is actually a spiral, with the first twelve letters representing the course from infinity to the relative world of matter, and the second twelve representing the movement from the world of matter back to infinity.

Do not be misled by the present pronunciation of each letter. The ancient way of pronouncing these letters was more like "Ahh, Buu, Shh," etc. These sounds enable you to penetrate ancient people's understanding. "Ahh" is equal to God, the infinite expansion; "Mmm" the most condensed, smallest world; that is why we say "Amen," or "Brahman," or, in Japanese, "Kami." "Ka" means "fire," or "power," and "Mi" means "water" or "body," so with two symbols, one yang and the other yin, ancient people made a word for God or spirit without any feeling of personification.

Let us consider the meaning of the first row of letters in

the alphabet. As we saw above, "Ahh" represents God or infinity. This more yin sound is followed by "Buu," which represents vibration, or the separation of the infinite expansion into two, yin and yang. In the sound "Shh," vibrations become yin, and diffuse throughout the universe; when we want to say "be quiet" (more yin), we say, "shh!" "Duu" is the sound of the spiritual world, as can be seen with words such as deity and demon. "Ehh" is the sound of physical manifestation, as with words such as earth, end, and environment. "Fuu" represents the sound of wind, "Ghh," the sound of thunder, "Hhu," fire, "Ihh," solidification, "Juh," water, "Kuu," a yang sound, for solid matter, such as ice, and "Lll," the sound of spiral motion.

Each set of twelve letters is grouped into sets of five and seven. In the first group, the first five stages correspond to the worlds of God, vibrations, and the spiritual and physical worlds, and in the next seven stages, their manifestation into elements such as wind, thunder, and earth. Then from M to X shows the return movement from the infinitesimal to the infinite through these worlds.

Try to discover the meaning of each sound by chanting the alphabet out loud. These sounds are called Kototama, which means the "spirit of words." But we cannot see this by the usual pronunciation; the original way of pronouncing the letters was the most simple. Therefore, read them again with their original pronunciations and meanings, and you will see a wonderful story of the order of the universe.

Figure 7: Oriental Alphabet

1/Infinity	WA	RA	YA	MA	HA	NA	TA	SA	KA	A	Infinity
	WI	RI	YI	MI	HI	NI	TI	SI	KI	I	
	WU	RU	YU	MU	HU	NU	TU	SU	KU	U	
	WE	RE	YE	ME	HE	NE	TE	SE	KE	E	
	WO	RO	YO	MO	HO	NO	TO	SO	KO	O	

5 Unmoved
Sounds

The Japanese alphabet also developed in ancient times and is based on a similar principle. In this ancient grouping of sounds, there are two poles on the left and right that uphold the upper level of heaven upon the lower field of earth. The old Japanese name for the "high heavenly field," or "Takama," was taken from the upper row. The lower line of matter frames the opposite side, and between these, transformations go. This creates four times eight, or thirty-two "children's sounds." This is the visible, manifested world; in between, the vibrating world is the sound of "U." "Kami" means deity, or spirit, and so this is taken from the top line; "Koto" means "thing," and so this is taken from the lower line of matter. The Japanese alphabet is something like an atomic chart, while the Western alphabet is similar to the story of how the world was made. To see the ancient world, see various alphabets and notice how each of them are telling part of the order of the universe in a different way; they come out like mandalas, Kanagi Guruma, and so forth.

Therefore, do not speak too much slang; words are the manifestation of vibrations and have the power to create our world as we speak them. When we eat poorly, we begin to speak slang. Friends who have been macrobiotic for a long time begin to change their pronunciation until it becomes very clear. Each word becomes nearer to what ancient people were pronouncing and to its original meaning.

Pyramids and Earth Energy

Before the axis shift of 12,000-13,000 years ago, the North Pole was pointing into a part of the Milky Way where thousands of stars are located. The spiral arm of the galaxy was more or less overhead between 16,000 to 22,000 years ago. The presence of thousands of stars over the North Pole made the night sky much brighter. These stars were sending radiation constantly to the North Pole, and that radiation was making the earth's electromagnetic belt and the meridians of energy that run along the surface of the planet very highly charged and active.

41

At that time, plants, including cereal grains, were very strong and energized. In a similar way, the human brain was also highly energized. At present, people use about 15 to 18 percent of their brain capacity. Even so-called geniuses like Einstein or Newton were using only about 18 percent. However, in this ancient time, people were using much more of their capacity, perhaps as much as 50 to 70 percent. Human consciousness was more highly developed, and ESP (extrasensory perception), telepathy, and the ability to see the future were common.

Examples of these abilities can still be found in modern times. In the mountains of Japan lived a race of people called the Eta. Their origin is unknown and they speak a very old language, parts of which resemble modern Japanese. One researcher who lived among them reported that they were living in a totally natural way, in complete harmony with all living creatures. After they harvested grain, they didn't mill or refine it into white rice or white flour. Like the Hunza and other traditional mountain people, they were essentially living the macrobiotic way.

One day, the master of the house where the researcher was staying went to town with plants, dried foods, and other items to trade. The trip took several days. Several days later, the daughter of the house was cooking a meal when suddenly she announced that her father was on his way home and was on a certain road about three hours from their village. She began preparing extra food for him. Then, at precisely the time she said he would return, he entered the front door. When the researcher asked her how she knew her father was coming, she replied, "Because I know, that's all. I know, therefore I know." Extrasensory awareness such as this was common in the ancient world.

In the year 2102, Polaris will come north directly overhead. Once this milestone is reached, we will start receiving more highly charged energy from the galaxy, and that will usher in a new era. Year by year, people's consciousness is becoming more and more open. However, since many people do not eat well, their physical condition and unfolding spiritual awareness are out of synch. In about a thousand years, we will enter a new world, charged by the same galactic energy that brought about one world in ancient times. At that time, people will become more sensitive to the energies of heaven and earth and begin to use them more productively.

In the ancient world, the forces of heaven and earth were used to grow food. Although on the whole, the planet was more highly charged than now, certain areas were less highly charged than others. Since plants depend primarily on the expanding force of the earth in order to grow, the key issue in agriculture is how to use earth's energy more intensively. Modern agriculture is oriented by science, and concerns itself with such things as soil nutrients and the application of chemical fertilizers. In the ancient world, however, people were more concerned with the flow of invisible energy, or ki.

Ancient people knew how to select the most ideal places for growing crops. They knew that fields situated next to mountains are strongly charged by invisible currents of earth's force running below the ground. (Mountains are themselves created and charged primarily by earth's expanding force.) In these places they planted crops that needed high energy to grow, and planted other crops further away. They also constructed natural generators that increased the flow of earth's force in their fields. They did this by placing large stones on the tops of mountains, thus blocking the upward flow of earth's force and diverting it down to the adjacent valleys.

They also knew that a very strong charge could be generated by placing stones vertically on the top of a mountain. When a large standing stone is positioned vertically, it acts like a huge acupuncture needle and attracts a powerful charge of energy from the environment. And in order to make the stone more highly charged by energy from the sun, stars, and universe itself, they polished it. They also cut small holes in the surface of the stone in which they placed crystals. Crystals are powerful conductors of energy.

Hundreds of these standing stones were placed on mountaintops throughout the world. Ancient people were also able to generate energy in places that were not near mountains. The charge of earth's force is much weaker in flat

43

terrain than it is at higher altitude. In order to collect earth's force in these places, they arranged large stones in a spiral pattern underground. The stones were connected to one large stone in the center. They also placed crystals in the center stone. The electromagnetic charge generated by the stones radiated in a spiral pattern across the plain, causing crops to grow very well.

Hundreds of these structures were built around the world. Today we call these "stone circles" and they can be found in France, England, Japan, China, North America, and other places. Depending on the area and the amount of energy needed, these structures varied in scale. They were very convenient and economical and many small villages could afford them. When the population increased, these structures gradually became larger and larger. They had to build more powerful ones. So they began to think it would be better to build a manmade mountain in order to generate enough energy to grow grains to feed large villages. In order to make a manmade mountain they developed a structure—the pyramid—that generated energy to the maximum degree. The original pyramids were flat on top and large stones were placed on their tops. The central part of the pyramid—especially the first third in height from the bottom—is where the most highly energized power is found. Electromagnetic energy is created there.

Again, hundreds of pyramids were built throughout the world. For example, near Tibet in a part of China that is now desert, can be found seven large pyramids. No one knows who built them or when they were built. The largest of these pyramids is much bigger than the pyramids of Egypt. The sides of each pyramid face exactly North, South, East, and West. Ancient people painted each side a different color and also used colored stones. The North face was painted black, the West, blue, the South, red, the East, green, and the center, yellow. The center and South are more yang and the North is more yin. These pyramids were built thousands of years ago and were constructed according to yin and yang and the five transformations. Of course, centuries of wind and rain have worn the colors down, but can you imagine how remarkable

44

they must have looked when they were new?

N

		Black		
W	Blue	Yellow	Green	E
		Red		

S

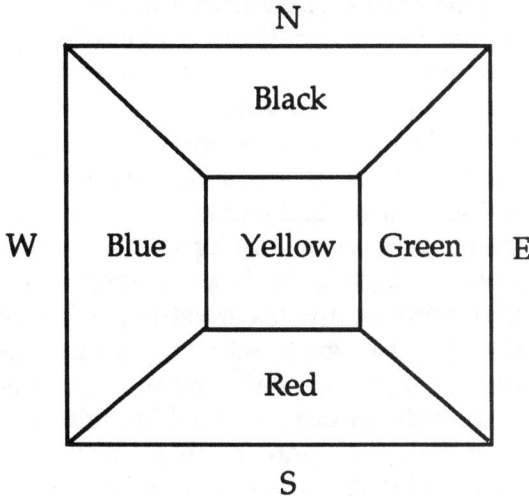

Farming Without Toil

In the golden age, people lived macrobiotically, that is, ecologically or naturally, eating cereal grains and local vegetables as primary foods. They obtained their food, however, in a way very different from present practice. We might call this "natural" agriculture, because they allowed nature to provide for them with a minimum of interference. There were four principles to their method:

1. Non-plowing. If we plow the ground in order to soften the soil, this can only be a temporary measure, because the rain will pack it down and it will dry, becoming harder than it was originally. This necessitates plowing again to loosen it, and eventually the soil's condition becomes like cement, requiring endless labor to maintain its viability. Thus, ancient people did not plow up the earth, but left it as it was.

2. Non-weeding. In modern fields, only one crop is planted; you will see the uniform rows of only corn, or only cabbage, and between the rows, only dirt. All extra vegetation that begins to grow there is weeded out with a great deal of effort. If we then go out into nature, we will not be able to find such segregation. There, many different types of life exist together. One type of grass may have shallow roots and another deep, so that they take moisture and nutrients from different levels of the soil. The roots of each variety of plant support certain kinds of bacteria, which work together to keep the soil healthy. When our more recent ancestors got the idea that weeds were not only useless, but harmful because they were "stealing" soil nutrients, the practice of weeding began.

This is the heritage of modern agriculture with its problems of soil moisture, bacteria, and lack of richness. In the jungle, no artificial cultivation is used, yet the soil is very rich, and a profusion of plants grow, all taking up balanced positions in which to share the sunlight and soil nutrients. Growing only corn, or only lettuce in a field is highly unnatural. Natural poly-cultivation, rather than artificial mono-cultivation, was used in the ancient world. The earth was like a garden that provided everyone with the foods necessary for life and health.

3. Non-fertilization. Because of the practices of plowing and weeding, the soil became depleted of its fertility. If only one crop is grown on soil, it takes certain nutrients out, but there is no other vegetation there to put it back. Usually, when fall comes, the weeds die and return to enrich the soil, in a repeating cycle of natural composting. If we harvest corn by carrying off the stalks (which occurs with machine harvesting), then after a few years we must either start artificial fertilization or move to another field. Without fertilization, the jungle and the woods grow vigorously, and likewise burdock and kuzu plants can be seen growing wild in great numbers. In non-depleted soil, fertilization becomes unnecessary.

4. Non-shearing. In a natural situation, the leaves of the different plants turn in complementary directions in order to share the available sunlight, their roots taking up balanced positions in the soil. Growing in this way, a perfect ecological balance is reached. Cutting off branches is the same as removing organs from the body through surgery. It destroys the natural balance of the whole and creates an unending chain of complications. Once we begin shearing, we must continue to work in order to keep it up.

Because of plowing, weeding, fertilizing, and shearing, farming came to require a large amount of work, so people either left the farm to live in the towns, or looked for labor-saving devices like mechanical plows and harvesters, chemical sprays, and automatic shears. Thus, endless difficulties were created, and as the plants became weaker under the artificial onslaught, the people who eat them also became weak.

Organic farming is by no means a complete solution, for organic food is not truly natural food. Artificial cultivation practices are still being utilized, although it is certainly an improvement over chemical farming. As we move closer to the style of natural agriculture employed in the ancient world, the farmer will be able to eliminate fertilizer, chemical or organic, plowing, weeding, and shearing, and probably even seeding, eventually. The only work left then will be harvesting.

Nature created human life, so in order for us all to be alive, in order for humanity to exist at all, there had to be a system of support already in place. If it had taken something other than this, some special creation, then humanity would not have appeared. If we are living in accord with nature, we do not need to slave all day long—this is artificial and unnecessary for our life. Archaeologists can find no record of organized, systematic cultivation prior to 12,000 years ago, so they assume that people in that era were primitive. In reality, they were much wiser than we, because they were using the gifts and powers of nature to the utmost, really working and living with nature.

Our life is playing and enjoying; hard work and sweat, worrying about taxes, in other words, the modern orientation of life, is wrong somewhere. Birds and fish do not worry, nor do they labor, yet they are well provided for. There is no reason we should be more unhappy than they. Of course, such really natural methods of agriculture will take many years to establish, since they have not been used for thousands of years. We must return the depleted, assaulted soil to its natural state, and this will take effort and perseverance. Each year, though, we will have less and less work until we have to work only two or three weeks of the year, and the rest of the time can be spent for enjoyment.

Ancient Treasures

Now let us see how ancient people confirmed star motions so that they could make them into such beautiful calendars and sciences of the heavens. At that time they also used instruments, but very simple and practical ones. Before the pyramids were built, they measured and predicted the motions of the sun and stars with three simple devices: the sword, mirror, and beads, which are still kept and remembered as treasures in Japan, although their original meaning has been forgotten and today they are regarded only as cultural symbols.

The sword was originally not a fighting weapon but a measuring instrument, as we can see from pictures of ancient ones that have been found. They were made of bronze alloy, and were shaped in a certain way, with a cross at the end of the handle, which would have made them unsuitable for fighting. Scholars think they were used for festivities, but they were not. In the villages, they were practicing natural agriculture, and they would place the sword on top of a nearby hill to sight the sun and measure the shadow it cast. In this way they were able to tell time and keep track of the changing seasons. The sword was never used for fighting. It had a wide blade that was much too dull to cut.

The mirror was round, with a design on the back that was similiar to the calendars and mandalas described earlier. It was also used to tell time and record the change of season. The front reflected light and could be used for making observations, like the sword. There were two types, one flat and the other indented or concave, through which one could see the position of the sun and determine the time of the year. The straight one could be placed upon a high mountain and used to reflect the sun into a village before it came up. Then the sword could be used to check the angle of the rays of the sun from the mirror.

As communities grew larger, and began to interchange, they needed central observatories to help whole territories at once, and so they made shrines, which originally were not religious. The gateway, or torii, was used to sight through to the shrine where the mirror reflected the sun's rays, so that the time of year could be determined. Cedar trees were used to surround the shrine buildings, because they stood very straight and cast straight, accurate shadows.

The beads were originally not used for decoration but for counting the days of the year, as there were 365 beads, eight with a special shape, to signify the solstices and equinoxes. Women were counting these beads every day, because of their monthly cycle of menstruation and also because they were concerned with seasonal changes as they affected cooking. Buddhist and Catholic rosaries later came out of this, but originally the purpose was very practical.

And so these instruments were called treasures; the sword, mirror, and the beads. After people began to eat badly, they became religious symbols, but in the beginning they were simple, practical devices for use in daily life. The pyramids are another example; they had holes in the sides through which the stars and the sun could be sighted.

Ancient people were living daily with the sun, stars, moon and with agriculture. When the sun rose, they arose and prayed to the sun. A festival for the Milky Way was held on the seventh day of the seventh month, July 7th. In autumn, there was a festival for the moon. There were various festivals, not only for the community but also for every home, which were celebrated together with the children. These were group festivals with nature, parties and celebrations every month and every week, and this, generally, was what ancient people's life was like.

3

Earth Changes

Soon the star Polaris will come over our heads, just as Vega passed over about 12,000 years ago, and a new world will begin. When Vega passed over, a great catastrophe arose, causing the death of millions of people and the destruction of various civilizations that had been built before this time. They were constructed about 24,000-25,000 years ago, and perished during the axis shift. After this, there were new North and South Poles, and a new equator. The axis did not shift a full 90 degrees but only about 66-67 degrees.

For some time after the axis shift, earthquakes and floods continued off and on for several thousand years. Gradually the earth became more stable, and new civilizations were able to develop.

Excavations of Sumerian and Mesopotamian cultures reveal traces of repeated earthquakes and floods, and repeated attempts to build up the civilization again. According to one archaeologist, one of these floods in the Mesopotamian region may have been the biblical flood of Noah. However, there was a similar tendency all over the world, and in four major zones minor earth changes were common for a long time; the Near East, the Far East, Northern Europe, and the West Coast of America. The records of these catastrophes are very remote and obscure, existing mainly in legends, but in the Japanese Kojiki, which was re-written only 1,500 years ago, a recent account can be found, which was taken from earlier documents remaining from ancient times.

"Kojiki" means "Old-events-book." The first part is mythological while the second part is historical; however, insight is needed to understand these records as they mention events in an obscure way. According to this story, there was a land known as Takama-hara; as we have seen, all of these "A" sounds represent a spiritual, heavenly world, and "Taka" means "high," "ma" means "space," and "hara" means "field," just as your hara or abdomen is a field of electromagnetic energy, or ki. Ancient people interpreted this as the sky, the infinite universe, and also correlated it with some place on this earth, thinking that we are somehow gods, and the order of the universe is working in us. In this place there was a goddess, Amaterasu-Omikami. Her name is made up of the words "Ama" (heaven) "terasu" (shine) "oo" (great) "mi" (beautiful) "kami" (goddess), and means "Heavenly shining great beautiful goddess."

As we have seen, the word Kami is an expression of yin and yang that is used to signify spirit or a deity, and is made from the sounds for fire and water. Ama is very much the same as amen. This is the way that words should be understood; by their sounds. Children everywhere call "mama" when they first begin to speak; Western people say, "He is calling his mother," and Japanese people say, "He is asking for food," but to babies, these words are the same; only the interpretation changes. In the same way, I am recommending Su for use in chanting, because this is the sound that a baby makes when he is asleep, while breathing.

Any language can be understood by sound; when you are a child you understand language that way, by catching the sound and trying to picture and form an image of what it means. When we eat the same food, our word structure may be different, but we can understand the meaning by sound. Here is a test to show how this works.

Speak these two Japanese words aloud: "yashashii" and "muzukashii." One of them means gentle, kind, easy. The other means difficult. Which meaning would you pick for each word? Try this now. If you picked "easy" for yashashii and "difficult" for muzukashii, you are right. Here is another pair: "yasai" and "niku." One means meat, and the other means vegetables. Which do you pick? If you think that vegetables are called *yasai* and meat *niku*, you are right. To take this farther, *nikui* means someone who is a hater, or greedy. The word *niku-niku-shii* means a very greedy, hateful person. This is something like "meat-meat-ish."

This way of understanding the spirit behind words is Kototama. It is the same way with words such as Brahman, or Amen; and also with words in languages which we do not know at all. Perhaps now you can catch the feeling of Amaterasu-Omikami and the wonderful land in which she lived, Takama-hara, a peaceful, happy place where agriculture was going on and where she was the leader. Her brother, Susanoo-no-mikoto, was a very mischievous god, with an earthy nature, as we can see by the "O" sound in his name according to the table for the 32 children's sounds that we studied in Chapter 2.

According to the legend, Susanoo returned to Takama-hara after traveling to many countries, and he began to do naughty things, such as destroying the fields of agriculture, and when people would fix them, tearing them down again. Finally he climbed onto the roof of a building where weaving was taking place, within which a girl was working, the heavenly weaving maiden named Ama-no-hata-ori-me (Heaven-of-field-weaving-maiden). Then Susanoo did a terrible thing; he threw a dead cow (meat) on this girl, and after a struggle, she died. Amaterasu-Omikami became so upset that she hid in the heavenly cave, and the whole world entered a period of darkness and many bad things began to happen. Thousands of wise people gathered and wondered how to bring her out from the cave where she had hidden herself. Finally they made a festival, so that she wondered what was happening, and when she peeped out a big powerful male god opened the door and pulled her out, and once again Takama-hara became a bright and peaceful country. The people deported Susanoo to the country of night.

This is a children's story; the maiden is the star Vega, in the constellation Lyra, whose death and departure took place about 36,000 and again 12,000 years ago, as we have seen. Before that the sun was shining, and natural agriculture was going on. This legend is most likely telling the story of the disappearance of the first one-world about 36,000 years ago, followed by a long period of darkness, and the start of the second one-world 12,000 years later. Unless we know the order of the universe and the phonetic meaning of words, it is difficult to interpret these legends correctly.

Global Catastrophe

About 12,000 years ago, the earth's axis shifted and the earth became as it is today. Before the shift, the polar regions and equator were in different places. Australia was formerly the South Pole and the North Pole was in the center of the North Atlantic. As a result, the East Coast of America was covered by ice, and the West Coast was warm. The climate in Europe was very cold. (The former poles are shown in the map as the circled areas.) Mongolia was hot, and so the people there and also the American Indians could move around very easily. The Eskimo were once living in a warm climate and could travel, and finally settled; then the climate changed, and they remained in the area where they are found today. Because of this difference, the western part of America had a much richer soil, and more rainfall. The coastline stretching from the northern part of South America, along Mexico, and up the West Coast of North America now has a varied climate, but it was once all part of the same general climatic zone, with mild weather, so that many people settled there.

Few people could live in the eastern United States prior to the axis shift, because it was very cold. The glacial ice made the underground become hard rock, so that today it is very rocky. When we take a ride in Manhattan we can see this, as there are many rocks everywhere. After the axis shift, the floods melted the ice in this area, but to the present time, the soil is shallow and not rich, and the trees are low, especially when compared to the higher ones in the western United

States.

In these times there were almost no people in Europe, and the few that were there lived in caves. Many traces of them have been found, including bones and pictures on the walls of ancient cave dwellings. They depended mainly upon meat and hunting because agriculture was not good there. Africa and the Middle East, towards Siberia, were warm, climatically fine, with many semi-tropical animals living there, including elephants and tigers. Later, people thought that these were the bones of dragons, and so they made many interesting myths. Actually they were elephant bones. India and Tibet were hot, so people wanted to live on top of high mountains to escape the heat, and that is why we find extensive civilizations built in such remote places.

Figure 9: Map of the World

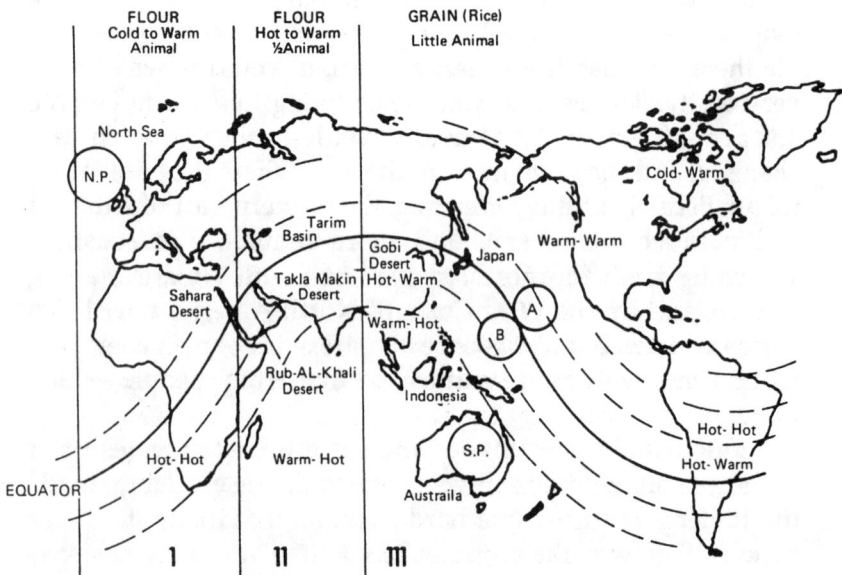

The deserts were once on the equator, but then moved. They are shifting slowly towards the south, except for the Sahara, which is moving towards the north, taking thousands of years. When the pyramids were built, the deserts had begun, but were not nearly as extensive as they are today. The Sphinx and pyramids are often covered with sand at present, but at the time they were built there was much less desert in these places.

The ancient one-world civilization developed along a belt above and below the ancient equator (shown as the solid line on the map), including Northern Africa, Tibet, Siberia, Japan, the Aleutian Islands, Alaska, Hawaii and the Easter Islands, and northern South America. They were eating macrobiotically, of course, and carrying on agriculture, raising mainly grains and vegetables. Because they were living in this warmer territory, their main symbol of worship was the sun.

The Next Axis Shift

In what manner will the next axis shift manifest? Whenever an axis shift happens, the leading and trailing edges change the most, and the more central positions change the least. In the last axis shift, the Atlantic ocean was the leading edge. It moved downward, while the mid-Pacific was the trailing edge and moved up, sinking the legendary continents of Mu. The middle regions of the North American and Eurasian continents were more central and changed less. When an axis change arises, it does not repeat in the same place as before. Therefore, we can predict two general areas where an axis shift might occur: (1) the eastern United States as the leading edge, moving downward and sinking, and the Far East moving upward as the trailing edge; and (2) Europe moving downward as the leading edge and sinking, along with West Africa, and California moving upward as the trailing edge.

You have read Edgar Cayce's predictions, but do not take these literally. You can correct them if you think his image is incorrect. Where will the most damage take place? Many people think that California will sink, but is this true? Some people are very busy; they moved away from California to escape this catastrophe, then moved back, left and returned again. Which will sink; this or the East Coast of America? Or the Far East or Europe? If California sinks, Western Europe will also sink; if the eastern United States sinks, the Far East will also sink. Study this with maps and think it over, trying to understand when the next axis shift will take place, the climatic changes that will occur, and where the belt of the future world civilizations will be.

There were two continents in the Pacific (circles "A" and "B" on the map) which had once been united but which had separated before the axis shift. They sank because the biggest shifts took place in the oceans, with the Pacific moving up and the Atlantic down. That is why the continents in these places sank and these areas became oceans. People could travel along the old equatorial line that stretched from northern South Africa to northern Asia, following trade winds and moving on land. This area was all one cultural block, as was all of North Africa and Asia. These were the two big land masses at that time. We may call them the Eastern Ocean Culture and the Western Ocean Culture, but they were closely related and interconnected.

Now let us see how the climate in each location changed. As we saw, Europe was more or less in the polar zone and became temperate. North Africa was hot and remains hot, while North Asia went from warm to cold. The upper Far East went from warm to cold, while Central Asia went from hot to warm. The West Coast of America was warm and remained warm, while Alaska went from warm to cold. The East Coast of the United States went from polar to temperate, while most of South America went from warm to hot, with the southern tip of of the continent changing from warm to cold.

With these changes, it was quite natural for eating habits to alter as well. In ancient times, people were eating more or less macrobiotically; with the shift, people who moved into regions that had formerly been cold, such as Northern Europe, had many difficulties. People settled in this area after the cold retreated; they wanted to eat grains, but the soil was poor, and so they could not. Today they can, but even until the medieval period the yield of grain was so low that it was not uncommon to receive back only one or two grains from each grain planted. Ten was considered an excellent crop. (In warmer climates, one grain could yield from eighty up to one thousand in return.) Naturally they struggled very much, and were forced to depend upon hunting.

Dietary Patterns

People ate different types of grains in different manners because of the climate in which they lived, and this made them have different ways of thinking. In Central Asia the weather was warm, so that they could eat good food, but because it was a continental location it was dry and grains such as barley, buckwheat, and millet were common. Here the environment was something like New Mexico and Arizona. China and Japan were nearer to the influence of the ocean, and their humid atmosphere made possible the cultivation of rice, which needs more water. Trade winds made the West Coast of America dry, even though it is near an ocean, and so the people there ate corn. In Europe people ate wheat, which is very strong and can grow in winter, and also oats and rye. But their problem was the toughness of wheat, which must be crushed before it can be eaten. The outer skin of brown rice is soft, and so people in the Far East could eat whole grains, as main foods, as we are doing.

Mentality comes directly from food. The people who ate flour naturally developed a way of living and thinking where everything was first crushed into pieces, as modern science does with the atom, grinding it into electrons and protons. In Asia, grain-eating people had an opposite mentality, where everything was seen first from the totality towards the small, and people who ate grain and flour both had a mentality somewhere in between.

Flour-eating people developed material civilization and science. Grain and flour people were more spiritual and somewhere in between. They were not so materially oriented as flour-eating people. Grain-eating people saw everything from the view of wholeness so they began to develop philosophy and principle. Flour-eating people were compelled to add animal food; grain and flour-eating people could eat less animal food; and whole grain-eating people developed non-domestication as the following story illustrates.

Soon after Admiral Perry came to Japan in the 1860s, the United States sent Ambassador Harris to live there. He and his people ate Japanese food but could not enjoy it, and so they requested of the government that they be allowed to eat beefsteak. When they asked for a cow, they were asked why they wanted a cow, and they answered, to eat. To eat! The Japanese representatives were astonished and replied that such things were absolutely prohibited in their country and completely against their tradition.

A great conference among the ministers followed, and they decided that this could not be allowed. When the negative reply came, Harris and his people were disappointed, and asked if they could not at least have milk, even if it were goat's milk. Again the officials asked why they wanted a goat. For milk? What will you do with it? Drink it? Again they were incredulous and held a big conference. Finally they decided to send a goat and see what these people did with it. When Harris and his people were milking the goat, the Japanese were watching, writing down the time and the methods used, and keeping records every day. Until only one hundred years ago there was no domestication in Japan. What a big difference this makes in the way people think.

After the great catastrophe, the world became divided into three main sections, and so people made sun, moon, and star flags according to this new plan of rebuilding. The star territories were those based around the intake of flour; the moon territories, half flour and half whole grain; and the sun territories were those where grains were eaten mostly in their whole form. Today these territories are becoming united, and we are returning to cereal grains and vegetables the usual, normal way of eating.

Ancient Maps and Alphabets

In Japan, there are a variety of old documents, including maps and alphabet tables that are believed to be many thousands of years old. They offer us a clue as to what the earth was like before the axis shift. In the map shown in Figure 10, we see a general outline of the continents, with some features appearing as they do today, and some appearing quite differently.

Figure 10: Map of the Ancient World ca. 17,000 Years Ago

7 HITOTSU- KUNI
Country of One

1 HIUKE- EHIROSU
Sun Receiving Country

5 AJICHI- KUNI
Country of Branch

6 YOMOTSU- KUNI
Country of Four Directions

2 HINATA-EHIROSU
Sun-Shining Country

3 MIYOI-KUNI
later Mu Continent

4 TAMIARA- KUNI

This ancient map is believed to be more than 16,000 years old, and is drawn in a very simple, almost childlike fashion, without many details. It shows the following territories:

North America—Hikue Ehirosu (Ebirosu), or "Sun Receiving Country."

South America—Hinata Ehirosu (Ebirosu), or "Sun Shining Country."

One of the lost continents of Mu—Miyoi Kuni.

Another of the Mu continents - Tamiara Kuni.

China—Ajichi Kuni, or "Branched Country."

Figure 11: Two Styles of Letters Used in the Ancient World

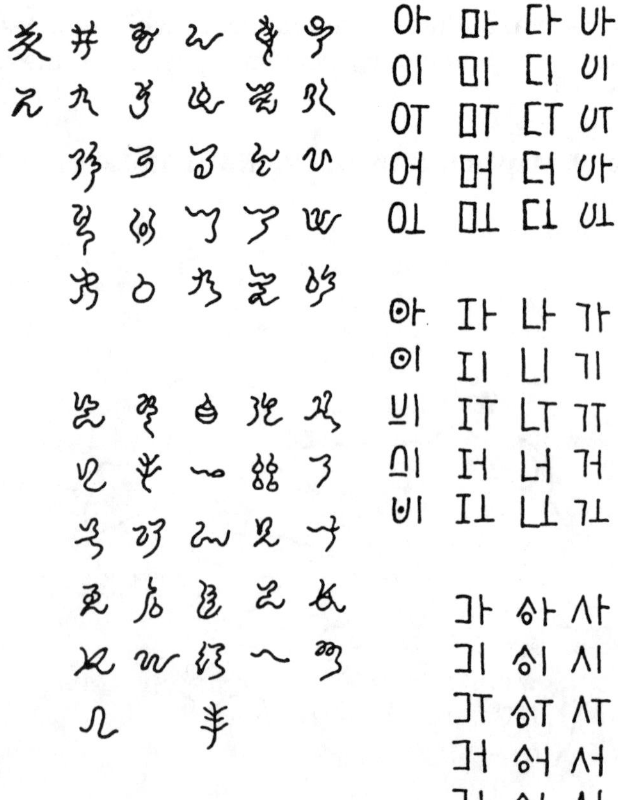

Europe—Yomotsu Kuni, or "Country of Four Directions," and also "Country of Night."

Greenland—Hitotsu Kuni, or "Country of One."

In Figure 11, we can see ancient letters. In the first table there are fifty letters, in the second, fifty-two. Although the letters are written differently in both alphabets, they have the same pronunciation. These are examples of the hundreds of alphabets that were used in the ancient world, all of them clear and definite, made in different styles. Some were made long ago, 50,000 to 70,000 years ago, others 20,000 or 40,000 years ago. Those shown in Figure 11 are more recent, about 20,000 to 24,000 years old. Some went to China, others to India, where they became Sanskrit, and others to Israel, where they became Hebrew.

These letters are the origin of the alphabets and languages in these and other parts of the world. Some look like the branches of trees, others like figures or faces, still others like the walking traces of birds. Ancient Egypt, Mesopotamia, and various places in ancient times all had different styles of these basic sounds and letters. We can see from the map and letters the simple mind of ancient people, and at the same time, their power to grasp the whole view.

Figure 12 (*see next page*) is a map of the earth as it appeared thousands of years later. If you identify North and South America, you can see a dotted portion where land sank into the ocean in the Caribbean. (The ancient character originally placed in this region means "sunk.") The other lands that sank or separated are identified, and the map also shows territories that were "born" or came up from below the sea. It seems that land masses under Eurasia, in the Indian Ocean between India and Africa, sank, and north of Europe, some land separated from the continent. You can see that the makers of these maps, who lived long ago, had very simple, whole-grasping minds, not detailed or analytical at all.

Through these maps and our imagination, after eating the food that was eaten by those people long ago, our native urge to become one family, society, and world grows. Since they were eating far more sound food than we are, they had a stronger desire for unity, and so "one world" was their motto,

Figure 12: Map of the Ancient World, ca. 7000 Years Ago

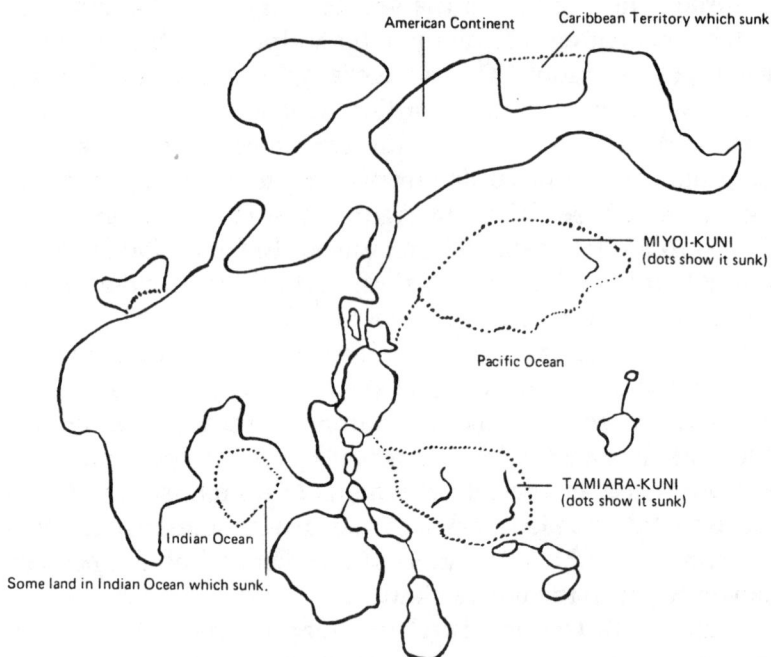

American Continent

Caribbean Territory which sunk

MIYOI-KUNI
(dots show it sunk)

Pacific Ocean

TAMIARA-KUNI
(dots show it sunk)

Indian Ocean

Some land in Indian Ocean which sunk.

and they made and lived in such a world. Present archaeology is discovering many things here and there, in Mesopotamia, the Far East, and in other places, but these are fragmentary discoveries. Scientists give names to these traces, calling them this kind of man or such-and-such hills, so that when we read of these things we are confused and cannot fit them into a larger picture. But if we have insight, we know that ancient people had the same kind of culture and were living in more or less the same way over the entire world.

Modern scientists are not eating the kind of food that ancient people were eating and cannot understand their cosmology and way of thinking. Scientific studies reveal the apparent material view, but we need to see the invisible mentality of ancient people in order to understand what their world was like. For this, it is necessary to have the same food and brain condition, and this can only be done by people who are eating whole grains as main food. They can penetrate the mind and cosmology of ancient people and know the common sense underlying all cultures throughout the world.

In the ancient world, culture revolved around 1) the use of fire for cooking and health of both body and spirit; 2) calendars and observatories, that reflected the order of the universe and that were used in agriculture; 3) the sound of words, which produced letters (there were many different alphabets, but everywhere the pronunciation was the same; there were about 3,000 different styles, but only 200-300 main ones), which made communication possible. To secure these: health, food, communication, and understanding of the order of the universe, government functioned as an information and educational center.

The ancient world also had a system of global transportation. There were big ships that could cross the present Pacific Ocean in about a month. There were also airplanes, which were much simpler than our own, which were called "heavenly floating ships" or "heavenly floating boats." They were powered by a simple mechanism which was commonly understood, and this, the sound of words, the universal principle and natural agriculture comprised the culture of the ancient world, including various festivities and celebrations.

Their philosophy was never to use more than they needed; they considered the earth, water, soil, and air as their mother, which, if it should be spoiled, would endanger their lives. Therefore, they used only the minimum necessary, and left the rest as capital and interest. They had a clear idea that the earth is producing every year, and that if the earth remains untouched, it will continue to produce. They never used the earth's nonrenewable resources, but tried to use leftover things, such as dead trees for wood fuel. Modern people have forgotten this and our planetary environment is now in danger.

Shrines were used as observatories and to understand the order of the universe. People felt automatically at one with nature and God, and they did not need salvation or paradise after death, because they already felt themselves to be one with the infinite universe, and their daily life was spiritual. But then the catastrophe came, eating changed, and suffering began, although some countries could keep their traditions to some degree. Minor catastrophes continued, and the observatories were changed into shrines. People lost their feeling of oneness because of poor eating and began to think that God was somewhere else.

People in paradise had freedom without the concept of freedom, health without any idea of what health was, happiness without the need to speak of happiness. They made symbols and designs, such as the cross or six-pointed star, to express yin and yang, but not as religious symbols. As an instrument, the cross was held up to check the sun's position, the angles of the stars, and the latitude and longitude. With this, they could see how the order of the universe was going on, as it was a guiding machine that anyone could handle, a direction signal, like a magnet, and when it was stuck upright into the earth it could tell direction by its shadow and be used as time-telling instrument.

All of these symbols were like this, not mystical or exclusive. The same is true of the Japanese chrysanthemum, or Imperial Crest. Like the mandala, the Aztec calendar, and other cosmological symbols, the chrysanthemum was known and used by many people. When a new world is built with the same immortal principle, we can begin to use these symbols again, or ones similar to them or can create new ones.

First we must establish natural agriculture; if you eat natural, not cultivated products, you become much stronger. We are definitely better because of our way of eating, but if we ate this way we would be much better still and could really know how food is the source of health and spirit. After you build up your health and understanding, you can help many others establish health and open the door to a new era. This is the biggest game I can think of so far that is worthwhile to put your lifetime into. It is so interesting that I would like to come back seven times for this thrilling, worthwhile, exciting adventure.

4

New Heaven, New Earth

We have studied the North Pole cycle of 25,800 years. Now let us examine it in more detail, according to the twelve divisions of the whole cycle. After the catastrophe of 12,000-13,000 years ago, some traditions remained in the places that were least affected, but the ancient world was more or less destroyed. Aftershocks from the poleshift continued until the earth finally settled into a new magnetic alignment. There were still minor earthquakes, even into our quarter of the cycle (the last 6,450 years of history).

The first 2,150-year period following the axis shift was an age of decomposition and chaos. Survival was the key issue, and people were too concerned with the day to day struggle for existence to think on a world scale. World transportation was cut off, and there were climatic changes, floods, and disruptions of ocean currents as the aftershocks continued. In the second period, known as the age of suffering, the earth began to settle down, and Europe, the East Coast of North America, and Canada—which had previously been covered by ice—became inhabitable.

The main problem facing people in that age was to secure enough food. Because natural agriculture could no longer be carried on, artificial agriculture, based on systematic cultivation, began, along with the domestication of animals and use of animal foods. People tried to enrich the soil and to pick up whatever they could eat here and there and to cultivate it as best they could.

We can trace agriculture to nine, ten, or eleven thousand years ago, but this is only artificial cultivation, not by wisdom or universal law. Agriculture began especially in Southeast Asia, the Middle East, and Africa, as well as in Europe when people started to move into the northern parts and change the wilderness into arable land. In order to accomplish this, a gathering force was needed, and rule by power and law began, together with war and battle. These developments gave rise to the third age, the age of power. Society polarized into governing and governed classes. Rulers used power and violence to consolidate control, and slavery began. These developments occurred about 8,000 years ago.

The turning point came about 6,000 years ago; halfway between Vega and Polaris, when the peak of the dark age was reached, and people began to have the idea of unification. This influenced everyone in some way, and during the fourth age, the building of huge towns and cities, empires, and huge stone structures, such as Stonehenge, took place, not only in Europe but also in the Far East. People did not know the principle yet, but began to think of unification and oneness. They tried first to accomplish this by power, and various kings and empires were created, and also mythologies telling about the past paradise. There were Greek, Indian, and other myths, and according to each, religions began.

Then, during the fifth age, these kingdoms and empires became powerful, and a type of oneness was achieved as commerce and trade developed and arts began. Greek and Chinese philosophy developed. The story of Atlantis appeared and triggered people's memory of the past one world. Life became more secure, but people were still governed by law and power. With more unified interchange, an international period began—motivated by the aspiration toward oneness. Various attempts to unify the world, such as the conquests of Alexander the Great and the establishment of Pax Romana, were based on power.

During the sixth, or international age, government and

politics developed from the local, to the national and international scale. Religions, such as Christianity, Buddhism, and Islam developed and spread throughout the world, as did ideologies and political philosophies such as democracy and socialism. Trade and commerce also became global, as did war and conflict. Science and technology conquered the whole world. At point "A" on the chart, humanity faced destruction by water in the form of the axis shift and great flooding that resulted. At present, we are at the opposite end of the cycle (point "B"), and face possible destruction by fire. Modern technology, including nuclear power and atomic weapons, is based on the intense use of fire in the form of energy.

Figure 13: The 25,800 year cycle

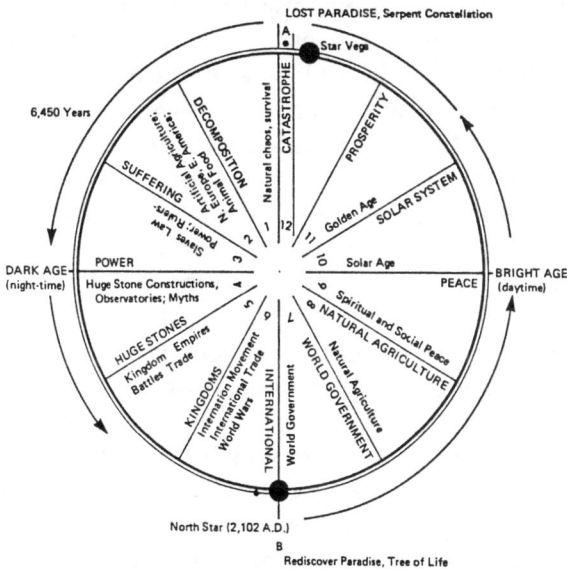

At the end of the fifth and beginning of the sixth age, Moses, Lao Tsu, Mohammed, Jesus, Buddha, Confucius, and other spiritual and philosophical leaders appeared. They, among various people, could see, because of their simple natural diet and self-training, that one world would come, not only socially but spiritually as well. Other people also sensed

67

this, but how, or in what form it would come, they did not know. These spiritual leaders saw things more clearly, and said that world unification would come, not through power but through love, or the "glory of heaven." Confucius called it "heavenly order," and Jesus and Buddha used other words, but they were all talking about the same thing, something beyond artificial law and power, and said that it would create a new world.

The Age of Humanity

In the past quarter of the cycle, war went for the purpose of unification, artificial agriculture grew, commerce, trade, and industries were accelerated, and scientific ideas developed to provide a dividing, opposite tendency to the unifying tendency of religion. Now, as we approach the end of this period, another turning point has been reached, all philosophies and ideas can be unified, and a new era can begin. If we consider the past 12,000-year period to be the dark, or night age, the dawn of a new, brighter age is approaching.

During the seventh age, or the age of world government, which we are about to enter, two approaches to world unity will emerge: 1) artificial unification through law and political and economic power, for example through such things as the United Nations; the European Economic Community, the "New World Order," etc.; and 2) natural unification by the order of the universe, or God's law, accomplished by people who have no power. The second type of unity will arise naturally as people's health and understanding are established, and out of this, a no-power government will be formed. Like government in the ancient world, the new world government will function as an educational, spiritual, and philosophical center. Power will shift from large, centralized organizations to the kitchen of every home.

"Govern" is actually a very poor word to describe this function, so please find a better one. During the coming age, the first type of government will show its defects and failures, and the second type will develop organically, together with the movement toward natural diet, health, and spiritual awareness.

In about 2,000 years, natural agriculture will be established on a world scale, leading to the eighth age. During that period, spiritualization will begin, freedom in the real sense of the word, for all of humanity. Artificial power and law will diminish, and finally natural order will take their place, leading to the ninth age of individual and planetary peace, and one unified world. In the tenth age, great technological development will take place, guided by the unifying principle, and civilization will extend into the solar system. The golden age will reach a peak during this time of interplanetary peace and prosperity.

The eleventh age, or age of prosperity, will come about 10,000 years from now. Wise people will appear to warn everyone that prosperity will not continue forever and that another catastrophe, in the form of an axis shift, is approaching. They will again teach the order of the universe; stating that everything changes and that whatever has a beginning has an end. However, because of prosperity, people will not listen much, and a period of decay and decomposition will inevitably come, followed by another global catastrophe. At that time, the cycle will begin again.

In the first quarter after the last axis shift, three natural divisions became established, as we have seen, by climate and environment, where people naturally ate flour, whole grain, and these two mixed. At the turning point which came at the beginning of our present quarter (about 6,000 years ago), these were made into three artificial divisions, by a conference of remaining macrobiotic people, to accelerate unification; then they scattered over the world and began to build each region. Let us develop Europe, Asia, Africa, South America, and the Far East, they said, and carried out their plan, making every part complementary.

Over the next several thousand years, this ancient dream will be realized and a new, unified world will come. It will take at least 2,000 years for this to occur, so I am not in a hurry, and do not need to achieve one peaceful world within one lifetime. However, we are presently approaching the turning point in this cycle, and now is the time to begin the transition to a new world.

To prepare for the coming paradise, we need to begin natural agriculture and rely less on artificial methods of cultivation. We also need to clear away misconceptions and delusions, such as believing that power equals justice, science can reveal ultimate truth, or that animal food is superior to plant food. We also need to re-establish the education of life, or Tao, and realize that learning how to maintain our health and live in harmony with nature, the universe, and endless change is far more important than accumulating information or technical knowledge.

Creating the New World

The forthcoming world is beginning now, and the modern world is rapidly declining. The signs are everywhere. The family—the thread that held society together from the beginning—is in a state of collapse. On an individual level, people's health and biological quality are also declining, as many degenerative diseases prevail. On the positive side, biologically strong people, a reconstituted species, are increasing throughout the world, and this is the meaning of the new world's beginning and the old world's ending. Our macrobiotic way is the soundest, most direct method for the new era. Below are some important points to consider when thinking about the future.

Food Distribution. What kind should it be? Organic, but also as natural as possible. Climatically, in the warm to temperate areas, the main food should be whole grains and their products, and secondary foods should be vegetables of the land and sea. Animal food should be one-eighth or less. Next, no one should pay for food. This is the source of life; we never pay the earth, the air, or sun, because these are the origin of life, and without them we would not be here, just as you did not pay rent when you were growing within your mother. Food should be absolutely free. Because the commercially oriented way came in, this was adapted to the food exchange, and accelerated to form cities. This is totally wrong if you see it from the view of the universe. Free access to staple foods is the first requirement of the new society.

At the present time, unfortunately, food must be charged for because the rest of society is doing this way. Natural food stores must pay rent and many other expenses. It may take several hundred years, but eventually everyone's food should be free, growing in backyards or available at community centers, whatever you need. Natural agriculture will minimize labor; it will not even be possible to use food as a standard of exchange, as rice was in Japan previously, because food will be free.

Land. Land should also be free. It is the mother of life, which we came from; societies oriented by land-ownership will continue for awhile, but eventually there will be no ownership. If land is there, the universe should own it. Use of land may be by individuals, communities, or groups; this is fine, but the idea that a person can own the land is so strange.

Education. I went to kindergarten for two years, grammar school for six; middle school was five years, but I finished it in four; college was three, but I finished it in two, university took another three years, and then I did five years of postgraduate work. These are the older Japanese types of schooling. Altogether I was in school from the age of five to the age of twenty-seven or twenty-eight. From the point of view of the universe, all of it was total nonsense. In the meantime I could not serve society and realize my dream. When such a long education is required to become a competent member of society, it means that society itself is wrong.

At the present time, education is oriented toward knowledge and technique. This is convenient and important, but much more important is how to live, what is life, how to develop health, will, love, freedom, what is nature and God; in a word, the education of real men and women, the education of Tao, or the way of life. At least one-half or more of education should be this kind of education, just as grains should be at least one-half or more of food. Mental food is similar to physical food in this respect. Then we can add knowledge, techniques, and so forth. In this new education teachers, more than anything, should be teachers of Tao. Their personality and way of life should really serve as an example to their students.

I have had many experiences living a wide social life in the past, and have met many people from a wide variety of backgrounds. I asked them questions. To a clergyman I would ask, "What is the Kingdom of Heaven? Where is it?" He could not answer. To a teacher, "What is freedom? What is justice?" No one could answer. It is strange. I made a list of questions, and discovered that uneducated people often answered them better.

When I moved to Boston in the mid-1960s, I settled in Cambridge with only four or five friends who had been studying with me when I came up from New York to lecture. I started giving seminars at Harvard University, but soon found that I had made a great mistake. They were not interested at all; they wanted only knowledge, conceptions, and data. Sometimes a professor would come; he could never understand at all. I wondered whether or not I should continue, thinking that perhaps I would get some result, but finally discovered that I had really made a mistake. I had wanted to give the most precious thing, using a department store; it is as if I were giving God, spirit, in Filene's or Jordan Marsh's bargain basement. They had come to buy underwear, socks, or cheap shirts, but not life itself. And so I lectured at home and began receiving whoever would come.

Education is a great problem today. The ignorant person in today's world may become the person of wisdom in the new world. Values will change; intellectuals may start to appear foolish.

When World War II ended, trade stopped, causing widespread unemployment in Japan. College graduates in leading companies were out of work; the juniors of the companies, who could do janitorial jobs or anything else, could still sustain their life comfortably. Then the leaders asked the juniors for help in finding jobs; but they did not know health and life, and could not live without the organization.

Macrobiotic education is the education of life, so wherever you go, without money you can live and develop your dream, give it to your children, and constantly improve yourself. Let us begin a kindergarten and nursery school, as there are now many macrobiotic children. Basic education should be finished by the age of seventeen, and then you should go out and gain experience.

At about the age of seventeen, when this Tao is finished, interest in the opposite sex begins; at that time, studying while thinking of boys or girls is difficult if not impossible. They should be free to choose then. In order to make education shorter, the method should be totally new and quicker to finish. Since people do not have this kind of principle, it takes longer to finish. For example, if you see the atom, what happens when heat is applied? Heat is yang, and so is the proton; therefore, the proton will change to yin. If the heat is small, it does not change much. As the heat grows higher, it becomes bigger and bigger, because it is becoming yin, and finally it would become unbalanced. You can see this without an experiment. Scientists found this out several years ago, the fact that the proton size changes, after building a billion-dollar research center and doing costly experiments. If you know yin and yang, such a simple problem is easy; since you do not know it, you need elaborate equipment, money, and time.

Art. Until the present, art has been showing the relative world. But when people awake to infinity, they will start to sense the absolute, invisible, spiritual world. Then art will change. How can the infinite, not the relative world, be expressed? If we have a sheet of paper, how can we express infinity? We may use figures, but, as a whole, it is infinity that we wish to portray. And so Zen monks used the simplest color, black, and most of the page was space. Then, with the simplest touch, they tried to show infinity.

At present, when one reads a book they go from words to words; in the future, they will not see the sentence, but the mind that composed it. Therefore, they will begin to read between the lines. When talking to each other, we listen to the words and take their meaning, but in the future, we will try to understand, while hearing these words, why this person is saying what he is saying, and try to understand his mind.

For example, you may serve a meal, and after your guest

has eaten, ask if he would like some more. In the United States, we usually assume that he actually does not want any more, and do not serve an extra helping. However, in the Orient, he may want more, but be thinking that if he asks we would be troubled, and decide that he had better not ask, so that we will not have to go to the kitchen or go to any extra effort. Therefore, when he says "no thanks," we must read his mind and understand why he said this, and say "Do not worry," and serve him anyway; or again, perhaps he really does not want more. This unexpressed mind is the true mind of man.

One of the reasons that you may be easily arguing among yourselves is that you are not reading each other's mind; you are too honest. Whatever he feels, he says; the listener also is honest, and hears and believes, both thinking that the front and back are the same; but through the front, we have to see the back. No may be yes, and yes may be no. When eating macrobiotically, you see front but also back, especially the person's mind and spirit.

Industry. Some people think that macrobiotics will lead only towards natural agriculture and primitive life, but this is not correct. Our idea is to use any kind of human possibility fully, as long as air, soil, and nature are kept in a natural, unspoiled state; but what we make, including arts and industry, should be developed. Otherwise, we cannot be creative. The only point is to make them more simple and efficient. In this way, even more advanced development can be achieved, as long as our technologies do not spoil us or cause human degeneration. In the future, the industry of change, based on the transmutation of the atom at low heat, low pressure, and low energy will become widespread, as will the use of free sources of natural energy, such as wind, solar power, and electromagnetic force, or ki. (For information on atomic transmutation, please see the book, *Other Dimensions: Exploring the Unexplained,* by Michio Kushi, with Edward Esko, Avery Publishing Group, 1992.)

Medicine. Medicine will become folk medicine; household daily food will be the primary medicine, while for more serious problems, these folk remedies can serve for 90 percent of the cases which appear. Only terminal problems or accidents may require the attention of the few professional people who will be needed. It will not be necessary to have thousands of hospitals and drug stores. In all of Boston, only three drug stores will be enough.

Other changes will come about automatically. Insurance will be unnecessary; the Prudential Tower will be empty. Military forces, which consume the national budget, will be unnecessary.

The marriage and and divorce system will be much freer, but the divorce rate will decline. The vast majority of couples, perhaps 95 percent, will have one to one relationships, while some will have more complicated combinations. Any form will be fine as long as the parties involved and their community are happy. Sexual habits will be more satisfactory, yet not so demonstrative or various, with more deep satisfaction, because the skin and mental development will be more sensitive, and although it appears quieter, the parties have more actual, deep satisfaction. Things such as X-rated films and pornography arise because people are insensitive; that is why they need such exposés and grotesque acrobatics. These will diminish as everyone becomes better; yet there will be deeper, harmonious satisfaction. The decomposition of marriage is largely due to impotence and frigidity, which will also be cured; and when families become more stable, this will bring about more lasting bonds among people, and society will also stabilize.

Trade and Commerce. These will continue more actively, but in a different way; they will not be the source of food and energy. To be happy and healthy we do not actually need currency itself, unless we want extra things; the more we need, the higher the price becomes. I am also thinking that in the future there will be one standard currency; but with regard to trade, since we are taking money, people are stimulated to gain money. If this were done completely opposite, it might be much better. Suppose you were buying a suit at a department store, and they gave you money. If you pick up a $25 suit, they would give you $25 and $100 for a $100 suit. You would have to spend this as quickly as possible, you would have to give it away.

If we made such an opposite circle, the poorest would be the best; the richest would be the poorest, because they would be giving the most. With such a totally opposite way, instead of paying taxes, the government would give to us; the next day we would start to spend. If at the end of a year, you had a million dollars, you would be egocentric; if you spent everything, you would be really wonderful, because you lived with the minimum necessary.

In these and many other ways, the future world will have various changes which you can picture. In order to develop your image, write an article about the kind of society you would like to have in the future.

Future World Centers

In Salt Lake City, there is a center for Mormon people; in Saint Peter's Cathedral Catholic people have their center, and Christian Scientists have a center in Boston. But as yet there is no center for mankind, no place to respect and honor the spirits of all people of the past and future. We need to establish a place where spiritually we can pray and make ourselves one with the spirits and souls of entire mankind, regardless of the cause of their death, and all of the people's offspring, together. If your father died, his spirit would be there; if you had an abortion performed, there would be a place for those aborted spirits. It would be a place where everyone could go and find their family, where everyone could feel oneness with their ancestor's spirits, and all of the other people who are in the spiritual world. This place should represent our cosmology, not through abstract symbols, but through things that can be used practically. It can also include an information center and school that could be shown to visitors as a model, where anyone could study and then go out to society and the world, making people happy and healthy. This would actually be a real world government, or our school, our community, our village, or our town.

There is really no such place devoted to humanity as a

Figure 14: The Main Shrine at Ise

whole. There were, when the ancient world had a community, many such places, but now there are none. We must make them; then friends all over the world can also make them, and can establish spiritual centers in each house, to respect their families, ancestors, and the spirits of all people. Let us begin to consider this.

Also we will keep good macrobiotics here and the people in that place will never change their way, keeping it for thousands of years, while the rest of society is changing its style of government, its leaders, and its way. When the coming macrobiotic world collapses in about 10,000 years, then among your offspring, some people would come out from here, reflecting on what their ancestors did, and again rebuild a healthy and peaceful world. So for them, too, we can do this, and leave our symbols and cosmologies; these can be by words, alphabets, and so forth, but also in the form of communities and central buildings, to contribute to the future world. It is better not to leave money and titles, but rather spiritual techings on the order of the universe, customs, language, farming practices, and so forth.

One rare remaining trace which ancient people built for that purpose is the Ise Shrine in Japan (*see Figure 14*) which is rebuilt every twenty or twenty-five years in exactly the same way as it was originally constructed. The uniqueness of this shrine is that it is made from wood and is devoted to agriculture. Farming is still being done there, to raise the best rice, to make the purest sea salt from the ocean water nearby, and this is devoted to the sun and to various aspects of nature and the spirits of ancestors, and is still being kept today as it has been kept for at least two thousand years.

Macrobiotic friends who have traveled all over the world have told me that there is no place like this, and that it has something unique about it which no one can quite define. We must build a new center like this, according to the principle of the order of the universe, and preserve our traditions for the future.

The real world center, that which I call world government, without power, can be built, and it is not impossible. While we are still active, let us build a spiritual and educational center and begin the practice of natural agriculture. When we do this, it will be the beginning of the new paradise on this earth, so let us do it.

The Tree of Life

As we saw in Chapter 1, the Book of Revelation tells the story of the cycle of constellations over the North Pole, and the effect these constellations have had on the last 12,000 years of history. Revelation also contains a description of the present age and the difficulties we are experiencing, together with a prophecy about the fall of material civilization and the beginning of a new world.

In Revelation, Chapter 15, we read, "And I saw another sign in heaven, great and marvellous, seven angels having the seven last plagues; for in them is filled up the wrath of God." In the Little Dipper constellation, there are seven stars, and these are the "seven angels." These were not in the skies in ancient times, but far away; and as the North Pole turned around its cycle, they came into view and now sit at the summit of the sky constantly, night and day in all seasons. This is a symbol of decay, the "last plagues" before modern civilization reaches its end.

Chapter 16: "And I heard a great voice out of the temple saying to the seven angels, Go your ways, and pour out the vials of the wrath of God upon the earth." These seven vials contain the troubles we are seeing now. "And the first went, and poured out his vial upon the earth; and there fell a noisome and grievous sore upon the men which had the mark of the beast, and upon them which worshipped his image." These are the various sicknesses which have spread over the world today—the modern plague, such as heart attacks, cancer, AIDS, and mental illness.

"And the second angel poured out his vial upon the sea; and it became as the blood of a dead man; and every living soul died in the sea." This passage describes oil spills and other contamination of the oceans and seas. "And the third angel poured out his vial upon the rivers and fountains of waters; and they became blood." This is the contamination of the waters of the world. "And the fourth angel poured out his vial upon the sun; and power was given unto him to scorch men with fire." Because the sun was darkened, we can see that this passage describes air pollution, including the increase of carbon dioxide and other greenhouse gases in the atmosphere, and also the development of modern weapons. "And men were scorched with great heat, and blasphemed the name of God, which hath power over these plagues: and they repented not to give him glory."

"And the fifth angel poured out his vial upon the seat of the beast; and his kingdom was full of darkness; and they gnawed their tongues for pain. . . . And the sixth angel poured out his vial upon the great river Euphrates; and the water thereof was dried up, that the way of the kings of the east might be prepared. And I saw three unclean spirits like frogs come out of the mouth of the dragon, and out of the mouth of the beast, and out of the mouth of false prophet. For they are the spirits of devils, working miracles, which go forth unto the kings of the earth and of the whole world, to gather them to the battle of that great day of God Almighty." These unclean spirits which come from the mouths of the dragon, beast, and the false prophet, are the false teachings and miracles which are now spread over the entire world.

"And he gathered them together into a place called in the Hebrew tongue Armageddon." Armageddon is not in one place and does not represent one type of war or destruction. Armageddon is war on all levels, and is beginning now. It can be seen in such things as the conflict between monism and dualism, men and women, parents and children, and old and new cultures and beliefs. These struggles will continue for about another thousand years, but the peak of Armageddon will come in about three hundred years. At that time, people who have the unifying principle and who have already begun to build a new world will not feel its effects.

"And the seventh angel poured out his vial into the air; and there came a great voice out of the temple of heaven, from the throne, saying, It is done. . . .And the great city was divided into three parts, and the cities of the nations fell: and great Babylon came in remembrance before God, to give unto her the cup of the wine of the fierceness of his wrath. And every island fled away and the mountains were not found." Here many troubles begin; this has happened already; the great World Wars of our century are described here; the things that we read in Chapter 16, the seven last plagues, have already been going on.

Chapter 17: "And there came one of the seven angels which had the seven vials, and talked with me, saying unto me, Come hither; I will shew unto thee the judgment of the great whore that sitteth upon many waters: With whom the kings of the earth have committed fornication, and the inhabitants of the earth have been made drunk with the wine of her fornication. So he carried me away in the spirit into the wilderness: and I saw a woman sit upon a scarlet coloured beast, full of names of blasphemy, having seven heads and ten horns. And the woman was arrayed in purple and scarlet colour, and decked with gold and precious stones and pearls, having a golden cup in her hand full of abominations and filthiness of her fornication: And upon her forehead was a name written, MYSTERY, BABYLON THE GREAT, THE MOTHER OF HARLOTS AND ABOMINATIONS OF THE EARTH." This "woman" or "harlot" is the spectacle of modern civilization.

In Chapter 18, Babylon is fallen: "And I heard another voice from heaven, saying, Come out of her, my people, that ye are not partakers of her sins, and that ye receive not of her plagues. For her sins have reached unto heaven, and God hath remembered her iniquities. Reward her even as she rewarded you, and double unto her double according to her works: in the cup which she hath filled fill to her double. How much she hath glorified herself, and lived deliciously, so much torment and sorrow give her: for she saith in her heart, I sit a queen, and am no widow, and shall see no sorrow."

"And the merchants of the earth shall weep and mourn over her; for no man buyeth their merchandise any more. . . And saying, Alas, alas, that great city, that was clothed in fine linen, and purple, and scarlet, and decked with gold, and precious stones, and pearls! For in one hour so great riches is come to nought. . . . And a mighty angel took up a stone like a great millstone, and cast it into the sea, saying, Thus with violence shall that great city Babylon be thrown down, and shall be found no more at all." With the casting down of this stone, the great half-cycle of the North Star is finished.

Chapter 19: "And after these things I heard a great voice of much people in heaven, saying, Alleluia; Salvation, and glory, and honor, and power, unto the Lord our God: For true and righteous are his judgments; for he hath judged the great whore, which did corrupt the earth with her fornication, and hath avenged the blood of his servants at her hand." This is what is happening now; sickness, crime, and mental illness in the fall of Babylon that we are seeing within our own lifetimes.

Chapter 20: "And I saw an angel come down from heaven, having the key of the bottomless pit and a great chain in his hand. And he laid hold on the dragon, that old serpent, which is the Devil, and Satan, and bound him a thousand years, and cast him into the bottomless pit, and shut him up, and set a seal upon him, that he should deceive the nations no more, till the thousand years should be fulfilled: and after that he must be loosed a little season." Refer to the chart of the North Pole cycle, and you will see that the constellation Draco is the dragon referred to here. Now the end of the cycle is coming, and the serpent is disappearing, so that the light from these stars will have no more influence. This period of a "thousand years" means "ten thousand years," or one-half of the cycle, during which these influences will not come; but after this it will return, and so it will be "loosed a little season."

"And I saw thrones, and they sat upon them, and judgment was given unto them: and I saw the souls of them that were beheaded for the witness of Jesus, and for the word of God, and which had not worshipped the beast, neither his image, neither had received his mark upon their foreheads, in their hands; and they lived and reigned with Christ a thousand years." "Christ" means the order of the universe. "But the rest of the dead lived not again until the thousand years were finished." This is the "first resurrection." "The rest of the dead live not again" means that for ten thousand years dualistic people will not come out.

The "resurrection" is often misunderstood to mean that people come out from the cemetery, but this is not correct; rather, the new world is resurrected by the movement of this cycle, and the principle of the ancient world returns and is reborn; this cycle is the resurrection. "Rise from the dead" means that past things come back. Because this is a poetic, aesthetic explanation, it is necessary not to take what it says literally. The mark on the forehead is not a real mark, but a sign of thinking power or intellectuality.

Chapter 21: "And I saw a new heaven and a new earth: for the first heaven and the first earth were passed away; and there was no more sea. And I John saw the holy city, new Jerusalem, coming down from God out of heaven, prepared as a bride adorned for her husband."

The "new heaven" represents the configuration of constellations that will come over the North Pole in the next half of the cycle, in the coming age of light; while the "new earth" symbolizes the peaceful planetary civilization that will arise during that time. The "first heaven" is the old configuration of polar constellations that appeared during the past twelve thousand years; and the "first earth" is the materialistic civilization that developed under their influence and that is rapidly passing away. The "bride adorned for her husband" is the star Vega, which will slowly approach the North Pole in the forthcoming half of the cycle. "New Jerusalem" represents the energy that the earth will receive from the galaxy during the forthcoming age, as the North Pole points directly into the belt of the Milky Way. This energy will charge the entire planet, elevating human consciousness, and making spiritual development commonplace.

"And God shall wipe away all tears from their eyes; and there shall be no more death, neither sorrow, nor crying, neither shall there be any more pain: for the former things are passed away. And he that sat upon the throne said, Behold, I make all things new. And he said unto me, Write: for these words are true and faithful. And he said unto me, It is done. I am Alpha and Omega, the beginning and the end. I will give unto him that is athirst of the fountain of the water of life freely. He that overcometh shall inherit all things; and I will be his God, and he shall be my son. But the fearful, and unbelieving, and the abominable, and murderers, and whoremongers, and sorcerers, and idolaters, and all liars, shall have their part in the lake which burneth with fire and brimstone: which is the second death."

"All who have fear, etc." are those who cannot live with the order of the universe, or their true selves. A long description of the heavenly Jerusalem follows, with twelve gates, and twelve foundations, twelve thousand furlongs in length, with the length and the breadth and the height equal, and the wall 144 cubits, with twelve precious stones, and twelve pearls, with no temple therein, "for the Lord God Almighty [the order of the universe] and the Lamb [the North Star] are the temple of it. . . . " The details of the new city's construction are exactly the same as the charts of cosmologies, Kanagi Guruma, and mandalas that we have studied in this book.

Chapter 22: "And he shewed me a pure river of water of

life, clear as crystal, proceeding out of the throne of God and of the Lamb. In the midst of the street of it, and on either side of the river, was there the tree of life, which bare twelve manner of fruits, and yielded her fruit every month: and the leaves of the tree were for the healing of the nations." In lost paradise, long ago, at the beginning of the Bible, humanity took the fruits of the tree of knowledge, and all of the troubles began which are told in this long account of history. At the close of the Bible, which is the present time, humanity is about to take the fruit of the tree of life, or the understanding of the order of the universe and enter a new world.

"And, behold, I come quickly; and my reward is with me, to give every man according as his work shall be. I am Alpha and Omega, the beginning and the end, the first and the last." This "I" is the order of the universe, the understanding of which is coming, leading to a new world built upon the principle of yin and yang, beginning and end, front and back, first and last.

We are now experiencing the last part of Revelation, and are entering into the city of the new world. Present occupations and people are passing away, and the new world will be built and begun by you. In order to prepare for the coming era, we need to (1) eat the traditional food of humanity— whole grains and vegetables; (2) understand the order of the universe, the eternal commandments, the tree of life, yin and yang, Alpha and Omega; (3) have endless appreciation and gratefulness for others, nature, and for the infinite universe, together with modesty and humbleness; (4) give our dream to others endlessly (one grain, ten thousand grains); in comparison to giving money, or clothes, which are small things, give yourself, your whole life; (5) always see, not only the front, the visible world, but also the invisible, spiritual world and order.

Everything depends upon your dream. When you have a dream, already, in the world of spirit, it is realized; it only takes time to realize it on earth. When you have a true dream, when you are eating well, definitely it will come in time. When it does come to the earth, whether or not you are still alive at that time does not matter, because it has already been achieved in the world of vibrations.

The dream of one peaceful world was imagined thousands of years ago in the ancient world. We have inherited that dream and will pass it on to future generations. The "biggest dream" means the most genuine dream that everyone has, of health, peace, and happiness. If you are seeing a true dream, you can enjoy it night and day and continue with it endlessly, both in this and in future worlds. This is the state of happiness itself. Each of us is assembled from the past. We are also the beginning of the future. The way we live today is what the whole future world depends upon, and will influence humanity for generations to come.

5

Spirals of History

As we saw in the first chapter, there have been thirteen epochs of history since the first human ancestors appeared on earth millions of years ago. These epochs are actually sections of a spiral, the center of which we are rapidly approaching. These thirteen stages, plus the center, comprise a spiral with seven orbits. Along with having seven orbits, the historical spiral can be divided into twelve sections, like a clock. Each section has a distinctive tendency that gives the events in it a certain character. These sections are explained at length in the book, *One Peaceful World* (St. Martin's Press, 1987), as is the historical spiral as a whole.

The spiral of history is winding inward. Each age is becoming shorter and shorter, while on the whole, civilization has become more yang and active. The speed of change is becoming progressively more rapid and we are using more intense forms of energy than ever before.

The speed of social change, or the speed at which we experience life, is becoming continuously more rapid as the spiral approaches the center. Events have been generally accelerating in a ratio of three to one, so that today, people are experiencing three times more than the people of the late nineteenth century, and nine times more than people in the seventeenth and eighteenth centuries. In those times, the pace of life was much slower and more peaceful. Our lives are about eighty-one time more busy than the lives of people in ancient Greece. Events are moving so rapidly today that everyone feels quite busy, even if they aren't doing that much.

Passing Through the Center

In about forty years we will reach the center of the spiral. That time represents the conclusion of the 32 million years of history. When the center is reached, humanity will go in one of two possible ways: either toward total destruction, so that the entire process of history comes to an end, or toward a new history as we pass through the center and continue in a different direction on the other side.

The spiral of history is centripetal, which means that it moves from the outside to the inside, and from the periphery to the center. It is governed by the forces of materialization. The more yang movement of history is making balance with our position in the galaxy. At present, we are approaching the peak of galactic winter. The solar system is furthest from galactic center and is in a more yin or expanded state. As a result, in order to make balance, human activity has become increasingly speedy, intense, and highly energized. Regardless of whether we are in a period governed by ideas or one governed by power, on the whole, events are controlled by materialism. If we pass through the center, however, a new spiral will be created that is moving in the opposite direction, from the center to the periphery and from the inside to the outside.

This more yin, expanding spiral will be governed by spirituality rather than materialism. It will also involve the twelve major tendencies, as well as more yin periods governed by ideas and more yang periods governed by power, but even with these, the movement of the spiral as a whole will be in the direction of spiritualization.

The question today is whether or not we can pass through this. Everything is converging at the center. In the next forty years many conflicting ideas will converge, and humanity will experience wars, revolutions, cultural decline, and personal and social decomposition. We will experience all of this and much more in the next forty years.

Today, there are now thousands of different theories about how to deal with cancer, and many of them contradict each other. And there are thousands of ideas about how to establish peace. People are arguing, trying to find their way through a maze of ideas; each person is pushing the others away and trying to become the center. But each person, each idea, is narrow and stuck. So who can really be the center? Who can pass through? The people who have the unifying principle, the whole view, the macroview. People who understand each individual tendency as part of the whole, who see all conflicting factors as complementary, and who are able to harmonize and unify them will pass through this time and create a new orientation for humanity.

Alternate Futures

After we reach the center of the spiral, we can go in only two ways. One is toward destruction, with all systems collapsing. This destruction will be by fire—modern civilization's technology is based on fire; energy is produced by burning coal, oil, and so forth. This center is very condensed and active, and as we approach it, our use of energy is becoming greater and greater—you may say this is a very hot civilization. If this collapse occurs by fire, by energy, by war, we must then return to the peripheral orbits of the spiral. As a result, humanity will return to a primitive way of life.

If we pass through the center without total collapse, we will not return to a primitive life but will begin spiralling centrifugally. The twelve major tendencies of the historical spiral will continue, but in a totally opposite way. Society will have a different orientation, and many changes will take place. Most importantly, our values would change into their opposites. Our present-day valuables would become worthless. Today, material things, like diamonds, property, and gold are given the most value. In the future, however, intangibles such as love, compassion, wisdom, and spiritual understanding will become more highly valued than material things. People will use entirely new standards to measure someone's happiness or worth.

Even if we pass through the center of the spiral, it will take time to accomplish one peaceful world. It will take time to completely change people's thinking and biological condition on a world scale. This will take time. After we begin spiraling centrifugally, we must pass through the first, second, and third orbits, and until we reach the fourth orbit—that means about four thousand years from now—the world will not be completely peaceful or unified. It will take about four thousand years of going in that direction before the whole of humanity will be able to enjoy the coming paradise.

From the beginning of the ancient world until now has taken about four thousand years—from about the twentieth century B.C. until the present. This has taken about three orbits of the historical spiral. The fourth orbit, before the beginning of Sumeria, Egypt, and other early societies, was the time of the ancient one world; that is, about 10,000 years before these early cultures began. About 30,000 years before that was also a time of one world. At that time, flying and other forms of global transportation and communication were common, and one language covered the earth, together with various regional languages.

After passing through the center, it will take about four thousand years until humanity has matured enough to enter one world. Of course, regionally and individually, people will become more and more qualified. Wise and peaceful people will start appearing with greater frequency. But, for mankind as a whole, it will take about four thousand years. The time of transition has already started. Two thousand years from now the world will be much, much different; society will be more or less oriented toward macrobiotics and the unifying principle. But for all individual people to be enjoying this one world will take about four thousand years, and this period represents approximately two sections of the 25,800-year cycle of the North Pole.

The Source of Freedom

We are now reaching the conclusion of millions of years of history, and are about to enter a new era. Humanity is coming of age in the galaxy, and all history up to the present has been a prelude to this event. The age of human freedom is about to begin. Let us now see where the key to human freedom lies.

Heaven's contracting energy is spiraling in toward earth from the universe, and earth's rising force is spiraling out from the planet toward space. The forces of heaven and earth run deep inside the body along a primary channel, or central meridian, along which seven highly charged energy centers, or chakras, arise. If the forces of heaven and earth were to run along an unbroken line, so that they were connected, we would be completely subject to nature, with no free will. However, there is one place where the flow of heaven and earth's forces is broken and interrupted: the space between the uvula and the base of the tongue. The mouth is actually the source of our freedom, and we can use this advantage in any number of ways.

Generally people are subject to the will of nature, as are plants and animals. Most people do not know why they were born, why they have the form they do, or whether their lives are predetermined or free. That is because they don't know how to use their mouths. Eating, breathing, and speaking—three activities centered in the mouth—create human freedom. If we manage them properly, we need not be mechanically subject to the will of nature, but can use heaven and earth for whatever purpose we like. That is the secret of freedom.

Until now, the overwhelming majority of people, including Beethoven, Gandhi, Freud, and other well known personalities, have been subject to the will of heaven and earth, and have been carried along by this spiral and its twelve stages of historical change. However, here and there, a few individuals appeared who could see the whole view, and who could maneuver in any way, whether they were living in the medieval or modern age or in a period of humanism or one of control. In any age, in any period, they were free. Mozart, Beethoven, and Goethe were produced people; a free person produces himself.

A free person may not be famous or influential, but he or she is actually the most advanced among billions of people. Such a person enjoys heaven and earth. He determines what kinds of food he should eat, what words he should speak, and what kinds of breathing he should do. And he determines how long he should live and what kinds of things he can do and enjoy in his lifetime, and how he can do them.

Daily food is the central issue in human freedom. Everyone is eating two or three times a day, and naturally that is influencing us physically, mentally, and spiritually. If we don't eat, we must die. In other words, food is changing into us; food makes us what we are and what we become. Yet, please read the works of past great thinkers—Freud, Aristotle, Hegel, Socrates, and others—and see how few noticed this simple fact. Yes, some noticed, like Jesus, Moses, and Buddha, but how many really understood what kinds of cooking, what kinds of cutting methods, or what kinds of chewing should go in what kinds of climates and environments, and how food governs our destiny? How many understood the profound significance of food?

What we presently call "macrobiotics" is the first biological revolution to occur since the appearance of homo sapiens on this planet. With the exception of a few rare individuals, humanity has only been following heaven and earth, and has been subject to natural evolution and natural degeneration. From now on, we can choose to develop ourselves or make ourselves decline. We can go either way, depending on what we want. That is the meaning of the tree of life prophesied in the Bible. Until now we have had ample opportunity to eat from the tree of knowledge, but have yet to eat from the tree of life. That era is now coming. After millions of years on this planet, humanity has finally come of age. Friends who are eating whole grains and vegetables and studying the principles of life are like the early pioneers. In the future, their way of life will guide humanity toward one peaceful world.

Resources

Kushi Institute — Michio Kushi Seminars

Studies in Destiny — In these ongoing seminars presented at the Kushi Institute of the Berkshires, Michio Kushi explores many of the topics discussed in this book. Included are fascinating and revealing studies of the way to see, judge, and freely manage both personal destiny and planetary destiny based on yin and yang, the I Ching, Nine Star Ki and Oriental astrology, the art of physiognomy and the art of placement and household arrangement. These residential seminars include macrobiotic/vegetarian meals.

Spiritual Training Seminars — These ongoing seminars presented at the Kushi Instiute of the Berkshires, are part of a progressive series designed to enhance each person's capacity for self-realization and fulfillment. They feature practice and experience and include studies of the ancient One World time, the Gospel of Thomas, the teachings and prophecies of Buddha, Jesus, and Nostradamus, as well as meditation, prayer, and chanting for health and peace. Spiritual Training Seminars are presented by educator Michio Kushi and feature simple macrobiotic/vegetarian meals with an emphasis on quiet eating and thorough chewing.

New Medicine for Humanity — In this series of seminars, Michio Kushi offers ongoing studies on the origin and development of health, the relation of diet and degenerative disease, and the reorientation of modern society in a healthier, more peaceful direction. These residential seminars include macrobiotic/vegetarian meals.

For dates, costs, and to register, or for further information, please contact:

Kushi Institute of the Berkshires
Box 7
Becket, MA 01223
(413) 623-5741
Fax (413) 623-8827

One Peaceful World

One Peaceful World is an international information network and friendship society founded by Michio and Aveline Kushi. Its members include individuals, familes, educational centers, organic farmers, teachers, parents and children, authors and artists, homemakers and business people, and others devoted to the realization of one healthy, peaceful world. Activities include educational and spiritual tours, assemblies and forums, international food aid and development, the Children's Shrine in Becket for the spirits of unborn children, One Peaceful World Press, and other activities to help humanity pass safely through this time.

Annual membership is $30 for individuals, $50 for families, and $100 for supporting members. Benefits include the quarterly *One Peaceful World Newsletter*, edited by Alex Jack, discounts of selected books, cassettes, and videos, and special mailings and communications.

To enroll or for further information, contact:

One Peaceful World
Box 10
Becket, MA 01223
(413) 623-2322
Fax (413) 623-8827

OPW Press Books

One Peaceful World by Michio Kushi with Alex Jack. Michio Kushi's autobiography and guide to a peaceful mind, home, and world community, hardcover, $17.95.

Nine Star Ki by Michio Kushi with Edward Esko. An introduction to Oriental astrology and cosmology and guidebook on love and relationships, health and travel, and getting through the 1990s, paperback, $12.95.

Let Food Be Thy Medicine by Alex Jack. Digest of 185 scientific and medical studies showing the benefits of the macrobiotic dietary approach on personal health, family health, and the environment, including diet and radiation, paperback, $10.95.

Standard Macrobiotic Diet by Michio Kushi. An introduction to the macrobiotic way of eating with daily guidelines and sample recipes, paperback, $5.95.

Fire, Water, Wind as channelled by Hanai Sudo. Divine prophecies of the Moon regarding coming earth changes and the spiritual practices, diet, and way of life that will help us pass safely through the coming storm, paperback, $8.95.

For mail order, make checks or money order payable to One Peaceful World and add $1.50 postage for the first book and .50 each additional book. For information on bulk purchases at discount, please contact: One Peaceful World, Special Sales.

One Peaceful World Press, Box 10, Becket MA 01223 USA

Index